Soliloquies in Solitude

Christian Heritage Rediscovered

The Series, as the name suggests, is meant to focus on Christian Faith & Living vis-à-vis topics like Literature & Poetry, Indigenous Philosophizing, Ethical Response towards Agriculture, Health & Healing, Science & Technology, Eco-Feminist Theology, Sociological Approach towards Human Rights, Law & Politics, Arts, History of Ideas, Ancient Civilizations, Cultural Contiguity, Religious Cosmologies & Mysticism, Footsteps of Famous Theologians, World Peace & Harmony, Global Capitalism, Network Marketing, Cybertheology, Population & Demographics, Epigraphic Studies, Contextualized Education, and many others. We welcome a Mss. on any topic/s mentioned, whether they are original works, scholarly monographs, collections of conference papers, revised dissertations, or translations of historical documents. Through the Series we, the Publishers, are striving to put forward published works that may help Institutions, Academic Bodies, Researchers, Scholars and the World at large in furthering their respective knowledge and understanding on the concerned subject. We welcome your comments on our efforts and further suggestions on how we can foster the upcoming thought provoking theologically grounded books.

Christian Heritage Rediscovered - 55

Soliloquies in Solitude

Solomon's Verse in His Nineties Depicting Cultural, Natural, Existential, Philosophical and Christian Themes

B. S. Moses Kumar

CWI

Christian World Imprints™

First Published in 2017 by

Christian World Imprints(TM)
Christian Publishing & Books from India
H-12 Bali Nagar, **New Delhi-110015**
info@christianworldimprints.com
www.ChristianWorldImprints.com
Phone: +91 11 25465925

ISBN: 978-93-5148-219-2 (HB)
ISBN: 978-93-5148-220-8 (PB)

Printed in India.

Contents

Foreword

At the 2003 Ecumenical *Kirchentag* in Berlin, I first became acquainted with some of the multi-faceted creativity of Dr. P. Solomon Raj. A large building at that event allowed artists from around the world to present their very diverse cultural expressions. It was, however, the colorful batik art of Solomon Raj that fascinated me most of all. Following up on a discussion held with his representative in Berlin, I made an email contact with the Vijayawada artist. That contact encouraged my wife and me to visit Solomon and Mary Raj in India, and to follow that visit with fifteen years representing his art at exhibitions from Washington D.C to London to Bethlehem. Only gradually did I discover that the Rev. Dr. P. Solomon Raj was truly a Renaissance man.

Much of the art work that was subsequently shared at exhibitions around the world depicted biblical stories using Indonesian batik imagery and both German and Japanese style woodblock prints. Both a Lutheran pastor and theologian, Solomon Raj was clearly fascinated with techniques that could proclaim the Gospel in visual form. Additionally, he had a deep appreciation for the way in which the Gospel could address the Dalit mentality in India. God's love as expressed in the life, death and resurrection of Jesus has a message for all who through sin have lost their ties with authentic living. Many already know themselves to be alienated, dysfunctional or disenfranchised because of sin. Yet Dr. Raj's creative renderings of women, refugees and impoverished people cause a viewer to ask, "Who is this God and why is he interested in me?".

With time I came to learn more about Dr. Raj and his need to share the Good News with everyone. He had experimented not only with batiks and woodcuts, but with wood, copper and bronze sculpture. He made etchings and worked with oil and watercolor. Upon occasion, he produced purely secular pieces but, for the most part, Pulidindi Solomon Raj was a preacher. He wanted people to know that God loved them and that Jesus was both their Savior and friend.

Additionally, beyond his work in the visual arts, Dr. Raj wrote plays and songs to dramatize the Good News on the stage and over the radio. He wrote scholarly articles in encyclopedias, chapters in books and whole books on the relationship between art and faith and on the cultural and theological meaning of Indian sects within Christianity. Dr. Raj has been a professor, a communications specialist, a translator and a chaplain. He is a husband, father, grandfather and great-grandfather. Could there be more?

To use a popular American expression based on a 1937 musical, about a singer who sang only one note, yet very well, Dr. Raj is no "Johnny one note." He is a true Renaissance man, who like other gifted polymaths, feels a passion to explore an interest in diverse ways. In his case, the passion is empowered by the Gospel, and no form of expression is off-limits to the preacher who, like St. Paul, can't be separated from the love of God in Christ Jesus.

With the publication of *Soliloquies in Solitude*, Dr. Moses Kumar presents yet another side of P. Solomon Raj. He is a poet who has shared many personal expressions of his faith in his observations of the world around him. To some degree, poetry is a friendlier form of creative expression for him because in his 90s he can no longer dip the batiks in the vats of hot wax. Nevertheless, there is aggressive and anxious power in the words that he pens while he and Mary quietly await their calling. We can be grateful to experience in these 127 poems one more rich outpouring from Dr. Raj who for so many years has graced us with intimations of God's love.

David Zersen
President Emeritus,
Concordia University,
Texas, U.S.A.

Preface

Life is a gift of God. We exist because of the breath of life the Creator God has breathed into us. He sustains and equips us until our last breath on earth so that His purpose for our lives is fulfilled and that we accomplish our God-ordained destinies. What we do with our lives is intended not only to be self-fulfilling but also to be beneficial to fellow humans. In the process, we bring glory to God as He delights in us and in what we do with what He has given. Conversely, people are gifts from God for the community we live in, and all the redeemed are gifts to the church and beyond. With mutual gifts and ministries given, we edify one another and contribute to the health of the 'body'. Dr. Solomon Raj is one of such unique gifts to the global body of Christ.

We see in Solomon's works an urge to tell – tell the gospel – in faithful response to the revelation he received and conceived. These poetic pieces came out from his heart and his pen in his Nineties, which he shared with one of his greatest friends, Prof. David Zersen. And, Solomon seems to have enjoyed the ensuing interaction pretty well from time to time. I had the privilege and double advantage of receiving them all to my file, as copies were marked to me, as well as frequent interaction on the phone on various pieces of his work. Some 127 such pieces were salvaged from my mailbox, which are hereby presented for the benefit of the reader. These poetic lines of Solomon's wisdom would never have seen the light of the day, but for the urge in my heart to collect them, ponder over them, and preserve them for posterity, for all their worth. These are now put together in some chronological order and thematic design. Literally, no one can perceive the length and breadth of this great and uninterrupted flow of imagination and thought – as he walked from his house to the adjacent Ashram with feeble steps during his sunset years.

We find here 40 Early Works, written from 2009 as an Octogenarian. He has titled this collection as *'Hridayanandam'*, which means 'Heart's Delight'. This in no way means this is Solomon's initiation into writing verse. Those who know him as an artist are quite familiar with his verse on every work of his art - a maiden reflection on his every art creation - written as a matching meditation. This exercise began as long back as his first published work of art in 1993 (*Living Flame and Springing Fountain: Batiks and Meditations*, Delhi: ISPCK), originally published in German in 1988. Apart from this, he is known for his excellent experimental works in many different Telugu literary forms. His other poetic works in English include *Songs from Sambalikan* and *Geetha Malika*. He is as famous for his pictures in art as for his word pictures.

When he began his life as a Nonagenarian, Solomon was into writing sonnets. Every student in India is introduced to sonnets, mostly of Shakespeare, in their graduate studies, if not earlier. This introduction initiates an interest in every student to experiment writing a sonnet or more, and then it remains an experience of their past. But, we see in Solomon an incessant desire to dwell more on sonnets even in his nineties. Having written some 12 sonnets in his early nineties, he composed 9 poems and three other sonnets in 2013. His later poetry contains a half of the present collection and is completed by the end of 2015.

By this time, he was fascinated to attempt another *prakriya* (writing process) in Telugu literature known as *Kandaardhaas* (A *Kanda* poem, taking the lines of a lyric at the end of its four-line composition). After this, he took up his latest experiment when he composed a *Vuyyala Paata* (so-called cradle song) in Telugu with more than 50 stanzas. Having been attuned to Solomon's bent of mind, I am challenged to preserve his 'Soliloquies in Solitude' for all their content and lasting contribution, and was inspired to do an analytical evaluation of this collection in this book. The actual pieces of poetry, numbering 127, are appended to this volume, so as to furnish the reader with a ready reference to my commentary, and also to make this a 'source-work'.

This is my penultimate tribute to Dr. P. Solomon Raj – as I reproduce the poetic works of his sunset years – celebrating his life and preserving his work for the church and for the global community. My ultimate tribute would be my forthcoming dissertation for Ph.D. in Theology with Sam Higginbottom University of Agriculture, Technology and Sciences (SHUATS) on *Incarnation of the Gospel in Indian Culture with Reference to the Art and Poetry of P. Solomon Raj*. With awe and wonder for His Grace, which has richly been manifested in his life, I pray that the Lord would continue to bless these lines for generations to come.

B. S. Moses Kumar, Ph.D.

Reflective Verse of P. Solomon Raj: A Critique

Introducing the poetic impulse of Solomon Raj is the task of the hour, and presenting a critique of his reflective verse is the need of our times. Solomon Raj of the Pulidindi clan, hailing from an obscure but picturesque village in South India, became a popular personality on account of his art in its manifold forms, or his writings – poetic, lyrical, theological or philosophical! Though from a family with meager means, the Almighty has showered His special favor on Solomon providing him with many means for 'flowering' like the ancient biblical king Solomon. And Solomon could reach some of the highest pinnacles in what he touched with his paintbrush, or in what he scribbled with his pen in Telugu and English!

The Poetic Muse seemed to have fallen in love with Solomon, without his knowledge. He therefore found himself, to his surprise, composing poems in Telugu, his mother tongue, from a very early age, and continuing in a diverse experiment in Telugu poetry, in spite of its structural complexity.

A) Solomon Raj: Literary Experiments

The journey of a poet began simultaneously with the journey of a priest. Having completed theological studies at Gurukul Lutheran Theological Seminary, Chennai in 1956, Solomon served as Student Chaplain thereafter at Andhra Christian College, Guntur for three years. Another year he served with the Christian Education department at Luthergiri. As aptly pointed out elsewhere:

> Discarding the traditional mode, Dr. Raj chose an innovative mode in his ministerial vocation. Never confined himself

to an appointed parish of limited horizons, but soared like an eagle with renewed strength and vigor the whole world becoming his parish.[1]

As an ordained minister of the Lutheran Church in Andhra Pradesh, he served with National Christian Council Audio-Visual Education for 7 years, with Suvartha Vani as Director for 9 years, and with Selly Oak Colleges for 12 years. All these seasons were like 'spring' for him emerging as a global artist-theologian, and evolving multifarious modes and models in art and literature. The present work is purposely limited to literature.

The year 1999 seems to be much productive since the following three literary works in Telugu were published in that year:

1) *Puja Mandiramu* (Temple of Worship), Vijayawada: St. Luke's Lalit Kala Ashram, 1999. Originally published in 1970's by Christian Literature Service (CLS), Hyderabad.

This is a *Dwipada Kaavyam*, verse written in couplets. It is rather a poetic expression of 'I-Thou' relationship between a devotee and his God. Solomon metaphorically names his heart as a 'temple of worship' with the refrain:

> Lord, I make my heart a temple
> To offer my worship to you.

2) *Veda Vinodini* (Scriptural Amusement), Vijayawada: St Luke's Lalit Kala Ashram, 1999.

This is a *Samasyapurana Kavyam*, with 100 metrical Telugu pieces. This is a unique creation with the last line of each stanza posing a riddle from the vast expanse of Biblical stories, and the answer is to be filled in the preceding three lines of the stanza. This work is a *Sataka* (a composition of a hundred or more poems) as well, with a difference! It is a unique literary exercise in Christian

1 B. S. Moses Kumar: 'A Biographical Note About the Author' in *Geetha Malika* by P. Solomon Raj (Delhi: ISPCK), 2010, p. 166.

literature presenting good humor and amusement in the acquisition of Biblical knowledge.

3) *Eeshodaharanamu* (Illustration of Jesus), Vijayawada: St. Luke's Lalit Kala Ashram, 1999.

This is a *Udaaharana Kaavyam* (Illustrative verse). This is an illustrative poetic exercise with a metrical poem and two songs, each addressed to Christ. It is a captivating call to Jesus on each of the seven case-endings in Telugu language. As such this is a very rare and high-class literary feat in Telugu. This work follows the great tradition of some great Hindu poetic works like *Basavodaharanam* of the Vaishnava poets of the 9th century rendered in the name of their deity, Basava. There was only one other Christian poet, by name Balli Purushotham, author of the masterpiece *Vishwa Deepam*, who brought out a Christian *Udaaharana Kaavyam* in Telugu, with the title, *Treikodaharanam.*[2]

Two other works were published as given below in the following years:

4) *Kim Kartavyam*: *Yakshagana Samputi* (What Task?), Vijayawada: St. Luke's Lalit Kala Ashram, 2001. Originally published by Amrutha Vani.

This is a collection of five *yakshaganas*, including the great dance drama *Kim Karthavyam*, which was staged in many cities of India. "It was really a break-through of all times in Indian Christian circles. Using the *kuchipudi* style, a famous local form of Hindu dance, known almost all over the world now, he created a unique form of communicating the Christian message".[3]

---

2 Dass Babu: *Andhra Christian Hymnal (Telugu) Biographies of the 29 Poets and their Messages* (Vijayawada: Global Telugu Christian Ministries), 2014, p. 298.

3 B. S. Moses Kumar: 'Liturgical Interests and Lyrical Innovations of Pulidindi Solomon Raj: An Experiment at Indigenization' in Praveen et al, ed: *The Yobel Spring*, Vol. 2 (Delhi: ISPCK/ACTC), 2014, p. 434.

5) *Gana Kusumalu* (Musical Flowers) Vijayawada: St. Luke's Lalit Kala Ashram, 2002

This is an anthology of 50 songs in Telugu set to music, and produced with orchestra and trained singers for radio broadcast. All these songs are "as fresh in depth and meaning today as when they were written … And this work is a culmination of Bhakti flowing through the twin stream of *sahitya* and *sangeetha* – beautiful verse put in melodious tune – refreshing many a wearied soul as they sing or listen to these songs".[4]

All the five above are five different and unique literary exercises (*prakriyas*), each requiring special skill and hard work. A concise description of these works, with their peculiar characteristics is given in *Geetha Malika*.[5] "Solomon's thirst for creative variety already kept him on higher pinnacles as a unique writer in Telugu literature, as he successfully employed different genres in each of his five published works in Telugu".[6]

The scope of the present work however is selective, and so is limited to the poetic exercise of his sun set years!

B) Solomon Raj: An Artist and A Poet

At the turn of the new millennium, Solomon turned out to be an octogenarian. His first major work on art, published in his 70's, majored on his selected 'batiks'.[7] This work contains 33 works. His further works of significance on art were published in his 80's: The first one in his early 80's presents both his 'batiks and woodcuts'[8] and it contains 29 batiks, 5 woodcuts and 3 acrylics all in color, plus 12 woodcuts in black and white. And, the second one in his late 80's

4 B. S. Moses Kumar: 'Bhakti Sahitya from the Heart of Solomon Raj' in *Geetha Malika*, op. cit., p. 94.

5 op. cit., pp. 92-93.

6 B. S. Moses Kumar: 'Thirst for '*Vaividhya*' in *Daiva Gnana Siri* (Vijayawada: St. Luke's Lalit Kala Ashram), 2012, p. 5.

7 *Living Flame and Springing Fountain: Batiks and Meditations* (Delhi: ISPCK), 1993.

8 *Fiery Wheels: Art Works and Meditations* (Vijayawada: St. Luke's Lalit Kala Ashram), 2003.

presents his hand colored 'etchings'[9] and this contains 66 works of Solomon's etchings.

Though he was into making 'icons' all along, they were not reproduced into print, but remained in their original state and elegance, adorning many centers of learning in several countries. Except for the icons, all the published works of his art invariably appear with a matching meditation – an instant, simple but profound piece of verse, emerging from his own initial personal reflection on his work.

Couple of his other works, obviously the very first and the last of his published works on art - significant for their serial form and nature - need a mention here. These are *Liberation in Luke's Gospel*[10] containing 12 color woodcut works, and *St. John's Gospel: A Gallery of Hieratic Art* [11] containing 13 color woodcut works - both adorned with matching meditations in verse for each of the works. The first work above was also brought out in Telugu, *Luka Suvartalo Vimochana Prasakti* in 2008, as a free translation from English, German and Dutch languages. Analytical evaluations by the present author on both of these works with art reproductions are available on the internet.[12]

C) Solomon Raj: A Lyricist and A Hymn Writer

As an octogenarian, Solomon could find time for more personal reflection and poetic expression. At the end of his 80's, in fact, Solomon could give time to render his collection of 44 *Gaana Kusumaalu* (Song Flowers) into English. They were the household lyrics in Telugu broadcast through *Suvartha Vaani* (Voice of the Gospel), the first Christian radio program in Telugu. Most of these and other songs by him were brought out in MP3 Compact Disc

---

9 *Etched Icons: Art Faith and Culture* (Vijayawada: St. Luke's Lalit Kala Ashram), 2009.

10 *Liberation in Luke's Gospel* (Vijayawada: St. Luke's Lalit Kala Ashram), 1996.

11 *St. John's Gospel: A Gallery of Hieratic Art* (Vijayawada: St. Luke's Lalit Kala Ashram), 2010.

12 http://www.artway.eu/content.php?id=1365&action=show&lang=en http://www.artway.eu/content.php?id=1366&action=show&lang=en

(CD) as *Golden Hits of Rev. Dr. P. Solomon Raj* on the occasion of his 60th wedding anniversary in 2006.

This author had the privilege of editing these works under the title, *Geetha Malika*, besides contributing an analytical commentary on the themes embedded therein.[13] Dr. Sumita Roy, an English professor at Osmania University likens them with the *dohas* (couplets) of Kabir[14] - a 15th century mystic poet and saint, whose writings have influenced the *Bhakti Movement* in Hinduism, and whose verses are found in the scriptures of Sikhism.

A manuscript in English with 11 songs written by Solomon at Sambalikan, the Asian Institute for Liturgy and Music in Manila, came to light in recent times. They were written with some musical notations during 1989-91, during Solomon's stay at Sambalikan as artist-in-residence. Dr. Feliciano, the head of the Sambalikan, was a Catholic and an expert in Western Music. He wanted to give harmonic tunes to these hymns but Solomon did not stay there long enough, and it remained a task unaccomplished. This collection of songs, however, was fortunately published in the Appendices of Geetha Malika.

The whole luster of this collection springs forth from the profound depth of the theological themes embedded therein and the rich imagery – Biblical and indigenous – which adorns them. The themes - of God's Protection, Man's Longing for God's *Darshan*, the Call of God, the Disciple's Response, Hope for the Future and the Final Destiny - were all woven well into these lyrics.[15]

In one of the songs, titled *The Mother Earth*, Solomon prays that God would teach us our responsibility in stewardship for the earth, and for everything therein. This is not only our obligation, but also God's expectation. In the concluding stanza, he expresses solidarity with fellow humans, as he confesses the corporate sins committed against nature. He seeks not only forgiveness for the sins

---

13 B. S. Moses Kumar, ed.: "Bhakti Sahitya from the Heart of Solomon Raj", *Geetha Malika* (Delhi: ISPCK), 2010. pp. 91-142.

14 "Foreword", *Geetha Malika*, op. cit., p. xiv.

15 http://docslide.net/documents/songs-of-solomon-from-sambalikan.html

of the past, but also asks for instruction and wisdom that would aid future stewardship.[16]

The ultimate outcome of this season in Solomon's life gave momentum to his further poetry, lyrics and Christian hymns in the following decade in both English and Telugu.

16 loc. cit., Quoted by Chilkuri Vasantha Rao: "Telugu Inculturation in Art and Literature" in David Zersen and B. S. Moses Kumar, eds.: *Planting in Native Soil: Studies in Gospel Inculturation* (Delhi: ISPCK & Autin, Texas: Concordia University Press), 2014, pp. 126-127.

1. Early Poetry of An Octogenarian

The first part of this present collection – "Early Poetry of An Octogenarian" – consists of 40 works, written from 2009 as an Octogenarian (in his 80's). He has initially titled this collection as '*Hridayanandam*', which means 'Heart's Delight'. This in no way means this is Solomon's initiation into writing verse. Solomon emerges, in his ascending stages of life, as a great poet in Telugu and English. It is true that 'man is a product of his environment', and as such we can locate the formative influences of a person in his surroundings – geographical as well as spiritual. The rural vicinities of the poet and the spiritual background he was raised in invariably reflect in his writings. The 'Early Poetry of An Octogenarian' depicts certain mundane themes, some religious themes and many philosophical musings, which are mostly didactic. Touching several things of every day life, which are a commonplace, Solomon draws his lessons of all times. And we also can navigate through his journey of life, as he moves from the mundane to the spiritual and on to the philosophical. He is as famous for his pictures in art as for his word pictures. Whereas his earlier poetry was mostly reflective verse – reflecting on the works of his paintbrush, instant and spontaneous, the present volume, is also reflective – reflecting on his memories and meditations on life situations, or *sitz im leben*, as the Germans would call it!

The poetry on the mundane themes is a poetic exercise of ordinary emotions and natural expressions. The poetry on religious themes is a confessional exercise of one's faith foundations. And the poetry on philosophical themes is personal musings on existential issues and concerns of life. An analytical survey of Solomon's early poetry, in the purview of these three realms is in order at this juncture.

A) On Mundane Themes

We find six poems on mundane themes in Solomon's early poetry as an octogenarian. The flora and fauna of this poetry portrays the rustic scenery and typical incidents of Solomon's formative years. An analytical commentary of these poems is given below:

First of all, the blessings of "***Deep Sleep***" and the ensuing rest and relaxation are mused upon. The Psalmist of ancient times declares that it is the Lord who "grants sleep to those he loves."[17] As we 'rest a while' with eyes closed, we lay aside all our burdens. And as 'a mantle of deep sleep' hovers on us, we need to 'stay a while' that way, anticipating a 'fresh dawn'. With a new dawn, we see a new path:

> The past has gone, it does not stay
> For you have now a new path to walk.

Having mused upon the natural blessings of sleep and rest, the poet ascends a new plane – here and now, and hereafter as well. In a companion poem, ***Heavenward Way***, Solomon muses upon not only laying aside burdens but dreaming 'holy dreams' – dreams that are given by a holy God. It is in deed a blessing to 'sleep peacefully' (undisturbed) until we wake up, and see 'the glorious sun once again' – the sun that does 'wipe away your saddening pain'. The dawn of the glorious sun that wipes away all tears also points to the glorious status hereafter!

In the poem on ***A Friend***, Solomon shares his musings on fluctuating times and fleeting friendships. He bemoans how a long time dear friend severed his friendly ties in spite of the many cherished times spent together and the joys shared singing together. Forgetting the story, though not easy, subsides all questions and the poet emerges with a foundational finding:

> … the bamboo flute
> Does not sing the same sweet song always.

---

17 Psalm 127:2, *The Holy Bible: NIV* (Colorado: International Bible Society), 1984.

In another poem on ***Paper to Write*** Solomon enlists the uses of paper:

> Paper to write, paper to read, roll away or wrap
> Or festival paper that many children wear as cap
> Paper on the kitchen table to wrap or mop
> Paper to write and paint on my tabletop
> Paper to beautify the living room wall
> Paper not to miss on the toilet stool.

It is interesting that the great 'story of paper' is graphically narrated in a few lines:

> ... Starting with parchment from the skin of a goat
> Passing through the weeds of the sunlit sea
> And other things like the skin of mulberry.
>
> Bamboo is great for paper of many kinds
> And the pulp of rice hay in all kinds of grinds.

Then the poet mentions about 'Chinese made paper' long ago he was told, and over the years of his full life how he loved to use paper for his pen and the paintbrush. The author vividly recollects how Solomon expressed his gratitude to his many German friends who helped him with 'rice paper' for his art works. For all this, the poet does "Bless the hands that invented paper" – the Chinese, "and India then followed".

There are a couple of poems on water. As Sumita Roy remarks, water is used as a recurrent symbol in Solomon's poetry.[18] One of the icons in St. John's Gospel was on the 'Water of Life' and Solomon acknowledges Jesus as "the deep fountain of Living Water, ever springing, ever flowing."[19] In ***Digging for Water***, the poet narrates the futile attempts of man digging for water to quench his thirst. All across the centuries till to date there have been efforts to dig for water, some successful and some otherwise. The poet laments the plight of the poor old man in the wood in the last couplet:

---

18 'Foreword', *Geetha Malika*, loc. cit.

19 *St. John's Gospel: A Gallery of Hieratic Art*, op. cit., p. 40.

> We do not know the reason why
> He struck no water for which he did try.

Even with all modern technology and know-how there are times when it turns out to be the same plight in certain places.

Another poem, ***Out From the Waters***, depicts the poet's personal plight as he crosses a fast flowing canal across a small wooden bridge, holding fast his grand mother's hand. As we see in certain rural areas, even these days, such bridges are often just the long palm tree logs across the canal. Having slipped into the waters and struggling for life with no skills of swimming, it's really a great relief to have survived. The author had a similar experience walking across the canal by means of a palm tree that fell on the bank. Those few moments of struggling for life, confessing all the known sins in the womb of the canal, seems like an unending eternity. But, hooray, what a relief in deed, when the feet struck the ground and we reach the shore safe and alive! Ruminating upon childhood experiences in the lines of poetry refreshes not only the author but the reader as well!

B) On Religious Themes

A walk through Solomon's poetry with religious themes is in order now. We find seven such poems in this section of the Collection.

The call of God in one's life is irrevocable and irresistible. The initial moments of the call were captured in the poem, ***I Heard A Voice***:

> A voice still and small
> Coming out from
> Somewhere deep

The recipient of the call wonders whether he was asleep or awake when he heard this voice, and wishes he had a piece of paper to write down the message. Though it remained just a wish, the fact of God's call was indelibly printed on his heart. Solomon in fact had a deep sense of God's call upon his life, and his subsequent obedience took him into many experiences in life and on to many pinnacles of achievement or accomplishment. It is interesting to see that there is a song from the Sambalikan, which Solomon wrote, with the same title, but with different wording.[20]

October 31, 2017 will mark the 500th anniversary of Martin Luther posting the *Ninety-Five Theses.* Hailing from Lutheran tradition, it is fitting that Solomon penned a poem on ***Faith and Works***, talking about the historic debate:

> It sounds so simple to the ear
> It is so difficult if we want to know its depth.

The question of the debate is clear:

> Is faith the fruit or is it the root?
> Does faith precede or follow good works?

When it became clear to Martin Luther, he tried hard to make it clear to us, as often men make some good 'works' and think that it is 'faith'. Solomon justifiably concludes that "If one can do good works all perfect" and "If we can do all that is needed without God", "Why a God"? and why "faith in such a God"?

Mere works of our human striving take us nowhere, but instead nurture in us a prideful ***Holier Than Thou*** attitude. In a poem with this title, Solomon portrays how he once saw a 'big fat man' in his 'soiled cloths'-

> With his raiment dirtier than
> The dust on the road on which he walks.

The irony of the story is that he demands "a little man who was also in a mess" to go and wash his dirty cloths. Through this incident, real or imaginary, Solomon projects the common proverb of a 'frying pan' that 'called the tea-pot black'. In fact, he concludes the poem with an analogy from Jesus' teaching in the *Sermon on the Mount*:[21]

> In fact the big man did not know
> That he was as bad as the other fellow

---

20 'Songs from Sabalikan' in *Geetha Malika*, op. cit., pp. 156-57.

21 Matthew 7:3-5, *The Holy Bible: NIV*, loc. cit.

Like a man with a big log in his eyes
Sought to help another with a speck in his.

In a similar vein, Solomon's poem on ***The Sinful Woman*** depicts the indignance of the self-righteous contemporaries. Apart from this common human attitude, the poet lucidly narrates how an anonymous sinful woman came to the Pharisee's house 'uninvited' to meet "the One who could wipe away her sins and give her a new life". She must be enacting the 'desired cleansing' in her life, as she "touched his feet, wept and washed them with her tears, wiped them with her tresses, and anointed them with great perfume breaking the jar".

Though "one person was offended because she was a sinner, and another man was deep in anger because the costly perfume was wasted", the Lord knew what she did and why and declared His perennial appreciation: "What she had done shall be remembered" - not her evil past but her redeemed present - "wherever the Good news shall be preached".

There are a couple of poems in this Early Poetry of Solomon on the crucifixion of Jesus Christ. In the first one, ***The Blessed Pebbles***, the poet describes the 'forlorn and forbidden' pebbles as 'blessed pebbles'. Though they were burning in the hot sun all day, they were 'moved with deep sorrow, wept sadly and wiped their tears' as Jesus "the prophet of Nazareth Came to that place called skull Carrying dreadful cross". The poet beautifully personifies the pebbles as they respond in sympathy and sorrow. The visible witnesses of Golgotha are the soldiers with their spears and the women covering their faces in agony.

The other poem on this subject, ***The Passing Experience***, presents the cross, the spear and the centurion. These are the "Sights we have in our memory's path from what had happened Long ago". But from here the poet moves on to our existential plight, where the cross and the spear can also be real in real life for some of us. They may not be manifested in a spectacular way but are silently endured "often kept hidden in the deeper Depths" of the passing experience.

Beyond the cross and the immanent agony and suffering, the poet finds the rays of resurrection and the eternal joys thereof. The poem, ***Resurrection***, is written with such hope and assurance:

When I go to my final sleep
I shall surely awake and rise again
And jump out of the pit
To go the way which Jesus had gone
I shall not be among the dead
Never to me a second death[22]
He sealed his promise with his blood
And that will be my second birth.

Solomon has incessantly expressed 'The Hope of Glory at the End of Life's Journey' in many of his other writings.[23]

C) On Philosophical Themes

Now we move on to the poems with philosophical themes, which consist of little over two thirds of Solomon's poetry of this decade. In this category we find three poems on birds and bees, six poems on trees and flowers, and four poems on day-to-day objects.

First of all, a study of "*poems on birds and bees*" is undertaken, bringing out the philosophical insights embedded therein. In ***A Bird in the Cage***, the poet portrays the inherent longing of a caged bird for praise from the visitors. It just wants appreciation for its wisdom, beauty and goodness – nothing more and nothing less! Such favor the caged bird found but for a while. Alas, there will be someone sometime, who is not pleased with us or with our performance. But this brings us enlightenment, deliberately or otherwise, as to realities of life:

... life is a mixture of good and bad as well
This, of course one day we all too should see
Because in fact that is what life should be.

Alas, the caged bird did not have courage enough to take it, and "It got a shock and fell dead in the cage". Any caged bird needs

---

22 "The lake of fire is the second death.
If anyone's name was not found written in the book of life,
He was thrown into the lake of fire" (Revelation 20:14-15).

23 "Bhakti Sahitya from the Heart of Solomon Raj", loc. cit.

freedom at some point, so that it becomes strong to take the good and bad of life. What a strong lesson for humans from this caged bird!

In ***The Sparrow and The Peacock***, the poet demonstrates how a sparrow envies a peacock, because of its beauty and the color. After all, the whole creation is marked by a rich variety of form and pigment. This poem teaches the need and importance to be content as we are created and endowed with. The sparrow learns this lesson only with the fowler's attempt to catch the birds with his nest, and when the peacock becomes a prey and the sparrow could escape. By means of this analogy, the poet, in the last stanza, conveys the lesson:

> A bigger mane is not always at gain
> Or a colorful plumage is good for the mien
> So thank God for the way you're made to live
> And never seek for more fancies and grieve.

This stanza is filled with simple but strange vocabulary. Mane means 'long flowing hair'. Plumage means 'a bird's feathers collectively'. Mien means 'a person's appearance or manner'. A long flowing hair is not always at gain or beneficial. Colorful feathers collectively are not good for one's appearance or manner. Therefore, "thank God for the way you're made to live" and "never seek for more fancies and grieve".

In yet another poem, ***Honey Bees***, the poet narrates the daily chore of the bees:

> Buzzing all around the trees
> Dipping into the flowery womb
> To get honey for the honeycomb.

But as they do their daily chore faithfully,

> Do they know the truth about
> What they're doing by and by
> To make the trees multiply?

Faithful commitment to our tasks accomplishes larger ends, knowingly or unknowingly!

Secondly, a study of about handful of poems on trees and flowers is taken up here with the philosophical musings therefrom. In ***Luxury of A Lovely Rose Garden***, Solomon depicts a pretty rose garden and the "joy of sweet flowers" and their flavors [sic]. The odors are alluring and as much as one wishes to spend there for ever, there dawns the reality at last, as penned in the last three lines:

> That life is not all unmitigated pleasure
> For man to enjoy as much as he may
> But life is both sun and rain in some measure.

In another poem, ***Transitory***, the poet endeavors to present the transitory nature of everything in creation, under the sun. The poet, as he walks along the fields and a lovely pool, gazes upon a lotus. This poem takes the lovers of poetry and lovers of nature to Wordsworth's poem on Daffodils, *I Wandered Lonely as a Cloud*. Solomon finds a great joy in the scene:

> ... I saw a lotus - in full bloom
> And green leaves spreading all around
> It scattered to winds all my lonely gloom

Lotus has a great symbolism for Solomon and he delves deep in its meaning and message – both in his art and writings. Beyond this fascinating experience, he confronts the stark reality of its transitory nature. When he revisited the pool for a fresh experience of its beauty, alas, it was a frustrating experience:

> Alas for me in the previous night's rain
> The lotus lost all its glorious raiment.

The poet not only captures this mixed experience but capitulates the purpose of frustration – not to drown us into gloom, but to take us to a new bloom of sublime prospects. The poet graphically sums this up in the last stanza:

> So all lovely things should one day go
> Leaving perhaps only an inward chime
> For, Nature had been designed so
> For us to enjoy new things from time to time.

In the poem, ***Lotus Flower***, the poet extolls the Lotus for all that it means to him, and for the rich symbolism embedded in it. We know in the Indian flora, the Lotus is the queen of flowers, enjoying the status of being the national flower of India. It brings to mind "symbols deep and sublime". Its course itself demonstrates great possibilities for humans to rise from the lowest depths and to ascend to the highest heights:

> Emerging out from the deepest darkness
> It rises up towards the sunshine's brightness
> Sprouting in time from it's dormant root
> Almost from death into life does it upwards shoot.

The poet salutes the lovely bloom thrice. Doing a thing three times indicate intensity and symbolize significance. Daniel prayed three times a day and completes the daily circle. Paul pleaded thrice for his thorn to be removed. The Lotus receives a three-fold salute for it symbolizes the answer for the three-fold petition of mankind, as found in Upanishads, and as recounted by the poet:

> You remind me of new life from deadly gloom
> To leave the darkness and rise towards the light
> Is to reach the wisdom's heavenly height.

And the poetic Muse takes him to imagine the presence of Lotus all over the universe including the Blue Nile River. The poet also finally pens in this poem that Lotus was the new material for his paintbrush as well.

The color woodcut of *The Lotus* adorns Solomon's second great work on his art.[24] Lotus is addressed here as 'glory of the orient' and as *shata patra sundari* (flower of a hundred petals). It relates to people of all religions and becomes significant beyond boarders. Buddhists read enlightenment in its face, and Hindu scriptures look at it as the *mandala* of the India yoga. Beyond its entire place in different religions, Solomon sees a message of eternal significance in the Lotus, which he communicates in the following lines:

24 P. Solomon Raj: *Fiery Wheels: Art Works and Meditations* (Vijayawada: St. Luke's Lalit Kala Ashram), 2003, pp. 70-71.

you speak to me of resurrection
of life from out of death
the resurrection of Christ
who conquered death
who had risen from the grave
and who can lead me
from darkness into light
from death into life.

We see a beautiful piece of art with rich symbolism on the theme of Christ's resurrection in this work. Thus he salutes this great flower – of a hundred petals and a hundred visions![25]

In ***The Sorrowing Banana Stalk***, the poet narrates the soliloquy of a tall banana stalk, which bemoans its fate, "Standing all day in the watery mud". It further laments:

To become mother bear fruit just once
And then to be cut up cast out by the fence
After that I am fully and surely forgotten
Giving my place to someone else then.

The pain intensifies and the agony aggravates when the banana stalk looks at the mango tree and compares:

Look at the mango tree, it stands
Year by year it its wide wing expands
Every summer decked in golden flowers
Perennially its sweet fruit it gives.

The banana stalk resents the perennial fruit-bearing potential of the mango tree. It further analyzes mango tree's potential, making it much needed for the "Bees to visit and birds to live", and even "Humans too desire its cool shade".

The poet narrates how 'the One above' responded, after hearing this inner grumbling of the banana stalk:

25 op. cit., p. 71.

And he decided to turn all the bananas
At once to turn into big mango trees.

And the outcome was neither desirable for mankind nor conducive to the order of creation and nature. The poet elucidates this situation in the last stanza:

But people did not want only mangoes
Which come just in summer days
But they crave also for the banana fruit
Which they can all the year round get.

Love the Trees is another poem that portrays the poet's love for the flora and fauna of his rural birthplace where he grew until his move to a city for higher education. He reckons and loves trees as his friends, for "they keep company with us in all kinds of winds". Solomon further remarks:

It is hard to imagine a tree-less earth
Trees are with us from our very birth.

This small poem is like an ode on mango trees! "I like to sit under my mango tree" – he writes, taking us to the poems we study in College, namely, *Under the Banyan Tree* by Glen Allen.

The poet further describes how he cherished eating mangoes – "I can never forget the taste of the king of fruits; it's not just his 'like', but invariably everyone fondly longs for the taste of mangoes before the end of every summer. In the last stanza, the poet could not but declare the rich variety of mangoes and their peculiar tastes, which are grown and cherished in his great land. Some of the household names are on his lips – 'name after name' like *rasalu* (juicy varieties), and *dil pasand* (heart's delight). Identifying with his fellowmen, he concludes:

We await the season for the mangoes to come
And we want to taste all of them or at least some.

One last poem of this period that captures his steps on the sea beach, in the woods, and upon the haystack is ***Alone!*** This poem presents the addresses of the places he frequented in his childhood, and which he recollects now with philosophical reflection. Sometimes, he was found on the sea beach seeing the sailboats with shells at his feet. Other times he was found in the silent woods nearby with 'the sound of the ominous bird'. Yet other times, he was found on the haystack – 'nice and warm in the early morning winter sun'. Having been immersed in the beauty of the season and the grandeur of the location, he often forgot to eat his 'fried nuts in the brown paper bag'. Recollecting all the moments of the past, he ruminates:

> In all this there is no lonely place
> However much I wanted
> For me.

Thirdly, we notice a group of four poems on certain general objects with philosophic significance. A small five-line poem, ***A Square Peg in A Round Hole*** is pregnant with rich didactic significance. This very much resembles the proverbs of the ancient wise man, King Solomon. The poet simply and clearly conveys that it is really hard:

> To put kind words in an uncouth mouth
> Joyful thoughts in a hapless heart
> And with kind words to mend a fool.

He likens this effort to "trying to drive a square peg in a round hole".

In another poem, ***The Kite***, the poet describes the common object in such a way that it brings out a common truth to the fore. The lovely Kite, in pretty colors, up above the end of the line, is personified and the poet imagines that the Kite perhaps knows the common truth – essential for all mankind:

> The string that holds together us both
> Helps us to be together in truth.

In yet another poem, ***The Signboard*** speaks to the viewers and demands attention to what it says. Only then its purpose will be fulfilled. It is a new invention and of course better than the primitive little string people used to remember their numbers. The essence of the poem lies in the couplet:

> I am not ashamed
> If ignored.

It is to the risk or disadvantage of the person that ignores the signboard, but the signboard itself is least bothered with such an ignorant or negligent attitude of the passerby. The poet alludes to Egyptians who in olden times used small pictures to send or receive messages, before they had hieroglyphics. Little things mean much when they accomplish needed functions, facilitating human existence and inter-personal communication.

Finally, we see in ***Door Called Dwar*** an analysis on door. This is pretty much like an ode, which is "a lyric poem, typically one in the form of an address to a particular subject, written in varied or irregular metre". The primary purpose of a door is well expressed in the first couple of lines:

> Door or *dwara* is a means strong and stout
> To keep us always in, and others out.

Further, we invite friends with open doors. In the second stanza the poet talks of three types of doors, intended and designed for three different purposes: 1) The garden doors keep goats straying; 2) Bed room doors keep Toms peeping; and, 3) Doors of steel (barbed wire and iron grills) to keep thieves out 'from mischievous drill'.

In the third stanza, the poet talks about keeping the doors open to our minds, so 'knowledge advent may happen'. The use of 'advent' here is very unique, and is a testimonial to the significant creativity of the poet. When our open hearts let our love flowing, our affection always will be growing. Open minds help us avoid prejudices, but open mouths cause conflicts. In conclusion, the poet envisages how the wise men pointed to us the importance of knowing "when to open the door and when to shut".

Door has been an important theme in Solomon's art and writings. The very first of the thirteen icons of Solomon from St.

John's Gospel is 'The Door'. The Lord is the door for all to go in and hide from danger – What a blessed door is the Lord:

> I come through the open door
> There is no fear to me anymore.[26]

There are also some fourteen other poems from this period on philosophical themes. First of all, we see in them a group of four poems dealing with some abstract themes and experiences. In ***Awake or Asleep***, we see an experience, real or imaginary, talking to a man in an indefinite status of awareness. We see here a couple of observations worth noting:

i) Some people see
What they want to see.

It may be far from reality, but they see something they want to see in others always. It is like everything appears dark to the one who sees with dark glasses.

ii) Some strange experiences sometimes stay with us longer, or forever, but other times they move on like a cloud. It depends partly on the person who keeps things within forever or lets them go!

In another poem, ***Light Sleep***, similar experiences are recounted. Light sleep - 'partly awake and partly asleep'! The things seen in such unconscious or subconscious status – "Is it all real as in real life"? Is it a lingering of a past experience or a forecast of things to come? Apart from raising many questions, the main question remains: "What is its meaning?"

In the poem on ***Darkness***, the poet presents the answer to the question of 'loneliness' and exhorts that "I need some good company in deed". But the legitimate question now is whether we can know in advance that a particular company is good. The complexity of the situation is penned well in the following lines:

---

26 *St. John's Gospel: A Gallery of Hieratic Art,* op. cit., pp. 28-29.

No, you have to test and see
How good the company be
Then if it's not to my taste
Can I leave the group in haste?
No, it is not easy at all
Once you in a bad company fall.

In yet another poem on ***Breath Control***, Solomon recollects one of the humorous experiences he encountered in his cross-cultural communication. While teaching Indian religions to a batch of teen-age boys and girls, he was introducing the topic one day on yoga practice. 'To practice yoga we have to learn Breath control', he said. There was a great confusion on the faces of his young pupils. On enquiry he knew that they thought he was talking about 'Birth Control' instead of 'Breath Control'. He just wanted to express his sense of humor in these lines.

Secondly, there are three poems on the philosophy of life. Solomon, in ***Life is Like A Train Journey***, likens life to a train travel. The train runs quick and 'people come and people go'. For some it is a 'happy journey' while others experience drudgery probably because of pressures and loads. Solomon observes the inter-personal exchange during travel, which is unpredictable: There may be a smile sometimes from someone, which is conducive for all to feel at home. Even if there is no smile, the journey continues and everyone reaches their destination. The lesson of life, we may draw from this, is even if we do not receive a smile from our fellow travellers, we can take the initiative in exchanging one, which changes the atmosphere: Sow a smile and reap a smile! What we sow, we reap.

The other two poems in this category are didactic and present the musings of the poet with the epithet at the end: "So said Solomon Raj" and "So once said Solomon Raj". ***A Trimmed Quill*** envisages the message to not find excuses but endeavor with the entrepreneurial skills one is endowed with:

Never say for a moment
That you were not born
With a trimmed quill in your hand.

To substantiate this invocation, Solomon presents couple of analogies drawn from universal truths:

i) "The tree had no fruits when it is planted";
ii) A sword cannot cut till it's heated in the fire and beaten with a hammer. Thus Solomon propounds that "A work of brain is half brain and the rest is strain".

In ***Seeking Support*** Solomon expounds the need to complement one another. Solomon enunciates the contrast between a tiny creeper and a solid tree, to show that "weak souls seek support". It is well known that "a solid tree stands on its own, like a seasoned oak tree trunk, facing all the rain and strain". With this analogy, Solomon exhorts:

Giving and taking some help
Is not unwise
Like a mighty gun will need a cartridge
To hit the target right.

Thirdly, there are six poems on the theme of virtues with a final poem on Solomon's 'virtuous woman'. Through the rural scenery of feeding the birds, Solomon portrays the virtue of gratitude in the poem, ***Thankfulness***. The poet delights to welcome the birds in the morning under the porch. And as he threw some grains, he could find crows, songbirds and others swarm around. As he happily observes them, he finds to his dismay that "they all took to wings and flew away" after pecking the grains. What delighted him most bringing a solace was the gratitude of the songbird:

But the song bird stayed on and sat in the garden tree
And started singing sweet songs for me.

In ***Love is Long-Suffering***, Solomon lucidly describes the long-suffering quality of love with a simile. In the few lines of this poem, he powerfully states that because of this quality,

> It does not jump to its feet too soon
> When things go wrong sometimes
> Love takes time to think and do
> Like the sun rises only after
> The night is gone.

In another poem, ***Love Reality***, Solomon describes another quality of love, namely, reciprocity or mutuality:

> Love is by definition, mutual
> One gives it and the other receives
> And the one who receives love
> Does also give it back
> Happily to the one who first gives.

At the end, the poet abhors 'self-love', as it turns out to be 'selfish love', and points out to the self-less fruit bearing of trees:

> But loving one's self is quite different
> It is that a person gives to himself
> Trees bear fruit but do the trees ever
> Consume their own fruit in hunger?

In a similar vein, Solomon condemns the selfishness or egoism in a small poem, ***I and Others***. As long as we find an equal or one superior to us, the egoism in us desires to puff up:

> I am the first and all others next
> So thought once an unwise man
> Only my opinion in the world is the best
> No one can think as best as I can
> But then came one better than him.

It is said that real Joy is when Jesus comes first, Others next and You the last. Waiting on others with the household words – 'after you' expresses it all!

In the poem, ***Company and No Company***, Solomon, as the ancient wise man, exhorts the readers to:

"Cherish the company of all your friends
Who come and join as the journey extends.

But we need to "stop fretting when they depart". They may leave us just like they came to join. During one's life-time, it happens again and again that "Some people join and some go away" until the end of life's journey, and "Till you yourself say goodbye to every friend". In the third stanza this status is graphically described:

Life's journey runs this way
Meeting friends along the way
One comes to you and the other goes
This is what life's experience shows.

The essence of the experience is summed up well in the last stanza:

Do not think that any one is unkind
Leave a sweet thought about every friend
Because all friendships are transitory
It is good to accept and cherish a sweet memory.

In the poem, ***Agree or Disagree***, the poet confesses his immature thought "that all should feel, just as I do and not differ a great deal". But very soon he found out "that it's not so easy to expect every one see just as I see". Even creation is rich in its diversity, and this variety is the beauty of life even among a couple:

We are not the same stuff all of us
Since creation was not planned that way
Different ways are the sole beauty of life
Also between the husband and wife.

The poet is emphatically nails this truth down with the analogy of a potter:

> If the potter made all pots the same,
> In size and shape color and name
> His would be a dull creation indeed
> To which really no one would heed.

The lessons learnt in life's observation are well depicted in the last stanza:

> So I have learnt slowly with a smile
> That others disagree with me once in a while
> Therefore it is wise for all people to see
> What the other person's opinions would be.

Finally, Solomon is fascinated to describe his own story in the poem, ***Show Each Other the Way***. The biblical image of marriage with complementarity as its essence is etched well into the lines of this poem. This sounds to be mostly autobiographical, with his story peeping through. The first two lines briefly and beautifully portray the start of his own wedded life:

> Once I saw a lovely little girl pretty and fair
> She loved me too and came with me her life to share.[27]

The theme of diversity is carried on even into this poem where he relates this dynamic from his marital experience:

> She agreed with me in life with all things most often
> But she had to differ with me now and then.

'Individual differences' are a fact of life and are very much woven into the human fabric, and they are never a hindrance even in the 'journey of life together'!

> This had never been a block to our mutual love
> Because we never thought of the one over the other above.

27 Mary Sarojini, the only sister of Balla Moses, whom Solomon married, and she was his tower of strength in all his endeavors and achievements in life.

The eternal purpose of diversity to be the complementing agent and completing element is beautifully summed up in the last lines:

> Two of God's creation each in our own way
> One always to show the other the life's way
> It is good for me to have some one to say-no
> When I sometimes, as often, go astray.

What a pleasant delight (*'Hridayanandam'*) Solomon must have as he penned these forty early poems as on Octogenarian! And what a pleasant delight these lines are to the reader, beyond their didactic contribution for all times!

2. Early Poetry of A Nonagenarian

The ninth decade of Solomon's life has seen greater pinnacles of achievement, though his global itineration has slowed down. His *Geetha Malika* was published as a Tercentenary Publication by ISPCK, Delhi in 2010. This work contains 44 lyrics. Though they were his own translations of his original Telugu lyrics, they turned out as original works, which accounts for his creativity and literary genius. Most of these lyrics in Telugu were household songs, as they were broadcast through the first-ever Telugu Christian Radio in Andhra Pradesh, in early 1970's. The present author edited the above work and appended some 11 of Solomon's '*Songs from Sambalikan*'[28] in this volume. Apart from these works in and translations into English, Solomon wrote a series of works in Telugu in his nineties.

It is rightly said that the pen and the paintbrush of Solomon Raj never seems to snooze.[29] Though the pace of his paintbrush had a slight slow down lately, the pen and the driving brain behind seems to have grown sharper. This may be verified by a couple of his latest writings at the threshold of his 90's, namely ***Daiva Gnana Siri*** (Treasure of Divine Wisdom), and ***Upamana Malika*** (Garland of Parables). The first work is released on Easter 2012 at Hyderabad and Vijayawada simultaneously, and the other work is later released at Andhra Christian Theological College.

'*Daiva Gnana Siri*' is an anthology of 157 four-line poems on 'Prayers and Proclamations' in Telugu. To these were appended 29 *Shashtyantas* - which makes this anthology a rare combination of

28 B. S. Moses Kumar: "Songs of Solomon from Sambalikan: An Analytical Review" in *Journal of Contemporary Christianity*, Bangalore, 2014 (Vol. 4, No. 4)

29 B. S. Moses Kumar: *St' John's Gospel*, op. cit., Back Cover.

his love for poetry and his love for devotional verse. And a couple of Christian *dandakas* at the very end makes it a rare and unique piece of Christian literature in Telugu. And, when all is said and done, Solomon Raj seems to be the only Christian author to have penned *Dandakas* in praise of Jesus Christ.

And, '*Upamana Malika*', also is an anthology on 20 of the 'Parables of Lord Jesus', in simple and beautiful verse in Telugu. Solomon very skillfully introduces or summarizes each of the parable with his profound reflection. This work may rightly be styled as reflective poetry. The shrewdness of his imagination, his simplicity in expressing profound truths from the Word of God, and, his 'thirst for *vaividhya*' are richly manifested in these writings.

There is another work published in 2014: ***The Hymns of Paul Gerhardt: A Free Translation.*** Paul Gerhardt was a seventeenth century Lutheran Pastor known for his voluminous hymn literature. The poet emphatically elucidates the necessity of the 'incarnation of the Gospel in Indian culture' here in these works, as he does in most of his previous writings and paintings. A brief analysis of the first two works above is made elsewhere[30] and is outside the purview of this present work.

The above three works were published as edited by Moses Kumar. Apart from these published works in Telugu, mention must be made of the unpublished works of his early nineties, mostly translations of hymns and poems from English:

i) *Adi Kraisthava Sangha Kirthana Sahityamu* – wherein 40 Greek hymns were translated into Telugu with a chronological account of Christian hymns in Church History.
ii) *Gerontia Swapnamu* – Translation into Telugu of *The Dream of Gerontius* by John Henry Newman.
iii) *Suvarna Dhaanya Sampada* – Translation into Telugu of *Golden Grains* by John Wright Follette.

As a nonagenarian, it is interesting to find Solomon Experimenting into Odes and Sonnets. Who never ever enjoyed an 'ode' or a 'sonnet',

30 Seminar Presented as part of Ph.D. course requirement at SHUATS, Allahabad, 2012.

as we come to study one or more of them in graduate studies, with a good English teacher who dramatizes those poems making them alive. I could never erase the dramatic portrayal of the 'Daffodils' or the 'Ode on a Grecian Urn', which remain still fresh in my mind after over four decades! One is no doubt inspired to try writing a sonnet with its particular meter and rhyme scheme. Solomon must have surely scribbled some such sonnets while in college. But it must have been an unfulfilled and insatiable desire as he took up writing sonnets again when he found time and solitude in his nineties.

Just as King Solomon of old tried and tested everything under the sun, Solomon Raj too seemed to have that urge to search the plethora of wisdom. One thing that we find, because of the consummation of God's revelation given us through Jesus Christ, is that Solomon Raj never said anything to be 'vanity'. But he sees the potential hand of God and His overarching purposes for man, as he set his hand on manifold projects of his life.

A) Journey Into Sonnets

The *Sonnet* was a popular form of poetry during the Romantic period in the history of English literature. Sonnets are fourteen-line lyric poems, written in iambic pentameter. Most of the Indian students must be familiar with at least one or more of the Sonnets of Shakespeare or Wordsworth – both April prodigies about 200 years apart! *Shakespeare's Sonnets* was a collection of 154 sonnets covering themes of the passage of time, love, beauty and mortality. It is interesting to know that he addressed the first 126 to a young man while the last 28 are addressed to a woman. William Wordsworth is credited with 523 sonnets while John Keats wrote 67 sonnets. Others known for their sonnets are Samuel Taylor Coleridge and Percy Bysshe Shelly – with 48 and 18 sonnets to their credit respectively. Sonnets - now in our times? Yes, it is interesting to see that Solomon penned some 15 sonnets that are available in the present collection, and he sure does revive our interest in this age-old recipe in English literature.

In this section we see some nine of Solomon's Sonnets, and the other sonnets of this period (namely, 'Liturgy', 'Troubles Come Together' and 'End of the Journey') are dealt with later in conjunction with related themes. Other 3 sonnets of 2013 are presented shortly thereafter. Sonnets, as we see, are ordered poetry, and these Sonnets of Solomon signify Solomon's ordered life and ordered confession – from natural order to spiritual order!

Solomon's 'Journey into Sonnets' began with a poem titled ***Sonnet*** - on his childhood exploits in the midst of picturesque rural settings. Solomon started his life in the nice vicinities, which he describes as follows:

Village life and milk from cows at the dawn
Small water brook in front of little house
Among others clustered in the green lawn.

He has friends and cattle for his time pass and merriment:

Some friends to play when it isn't school time
Or graze the cattle in midday hot sun
Singing folk songs of joy and dance to rhyme
Chasing each other and then on to run.

Raj comes always somewhat late for his lunch, unless he is away on a long trip; or ran away to the beach, with all his friends, to see on the sea a sailing new ship. This is the way they spent life happily, but, with a sincere realization in the last line: "Raj and his friends escaped proper tending".

In another autobiographical sonnet, ***A Village Boy***, he describes himself as a happy village boy –

Jumping playing swimming at the seashore
Climbing trees and picking fruits in plenty

- never caring for any thing! His attachment to the nature and the things around are portrayed with gratitude for these gifts from above:

The earth, the sun, the wind and water cool
The calf and cow the grassy fields I love …
These are the gifts we all get from above.

We always cherish these gifts of God in gratitude. The one who is blind to these is surely poor and misses much joy, and his life becomes dull and sad. Solomon extols God for His 'sweet creation' and thanks Him as 'He made us prosperous'!

In another sonnet, Solomon shares his philosophical musings on ***Adwaitha***, which means Monism or non-dual Oneness. The reasoning and questioning faculties are at their best as he contemplates about being 'united with God'. Is it a hereafter thing or 'here and now' thing? When all is said and done, Solomon propounds the proposition of real 'oneness with God':

True *aikya* should happen on earth truly
In prayer and constant meditation
This leads to the oneness with the Holy
God is God and man is nothing but man.

Finally, it is desirable and feasible that "God is to be enjoyed like sweet sugar". As things stand as they are, Solomon questions: "what joy if man himself becomes sugar"? Having concluded the debate in all the lines of the sonnet, Solomon states his preference in parenthesis:

(So I like 'I and thou' relationship with God
Rather than being lost in him)!

He wrote another sonnet on ***The Alcoholic***, one of the social evils of all times. It is a common thing for rustic folks to become enslaved by cheap liquor. The intoxication temporarily helps them forget all the cares and loads of life. They are after this for an easy escape from all trouble. Solomon addressed other social evils later in some seven poems. Giving a thought to the evil consequences of this addiction, he addresses and exhorts the alcoholic in these lines:

Foolish man drowning deep in alcohol
You lose your senses and forget your shame
Do you know that what you earn is bad name?
Open your eyes before turning a fool.

Losing sense, the alcoholic immerses in all sorts of demeaning actions, earning nothing but a bad name. Solomon makes a plea in the following lines to pause and think about the value of life and then to mend the way:

Can't you pause in your life a while and think?
Life should never become a wasted game
Better kill your passions, bring them to tame
Before you soon in a deadly pit sink.

This causes "pain to parents and the partner", haunting life-long 'like a big ghost', with no peace on the deathbed. The final fate 'in endless flames' is to be lost "in the name of a wicked and poor drunkard" - 'unwept unsung and unremembered'. There is an allusion in the last line to 'The Lay of the Last Minstrel' by Sir Walter Scott, where the fate of an unpatriotic person is penned: "Unwept, unhonored and unsung".

In the sonnet on ***Early Rising***, Solomon brings out the utility of the primitive saying, "Early to bed and early too to rise":

We're sure this saying was not meant for fun
By this during day more work could be done
And so this to us is not a mighty surprise.

The lifestyle of the older generations was fashioned by this, as they were committed to this simple rule, "Whether this made them healthy, wealthy, wise". With the changing times the changing habits are in vogue. Solomon is considerate to this and sees this as an optional, and concludes that life needs to be lived happily instead of becoming drudgery:

Lifestyles have drastically changed so
Nighttime is so pleasant to some people
To rise with the sun to them is trouble
I guess life has to be happily lived also.

After all, "Early to rise is not a big gospel" Solomon says, and "To stick to this old rule is impossible".

Another sonnet, ***Two Kinds of Friendship***, deals with Friendship, and distinguishes godly friendship with worldly friendship:

God-fearing friends are always good to have
For counseling and for time for prayer too …

To pray with fellow believers is bliss
With God to spend some time with them is good
So that they and you to each other wish
His love and abundant peace and sainthood.

Extolling godly friendship for the outcome of counseling, prayer and fellowship and for the emerging fruit of love, peace and sainthood, Solomon warns about the 'worldly chatting' - 'Which create rivalries and sadness too'. The last couplet graphically portrays the distinction between the two:

"Believers do bring glory to His name
Worldly assemblies are another game".

The sonnet on ***Giving and Receiving*** vividly presents the Biblical message of 'giving' – even the supreme giving Himself of the Son of God! This sounds a 'confessional' proclaiming the tenets of Christian faith. The Christian lifestyle of giving is manifested in the first couple of lines:

We help others in need and this we know
'Tis more blessed to give than to receive.

Here is an allusion to the Biblical reference of Acts 20:35. The spiritual gifts of giving and benevolence are emphasized: "We give ourselves to God and too alms give". Giving implies giving to God (beyond His tithe), and benevolence is giving to those in need! The Gospel of Giving is well portrayed in the next stanza:

The Son of God gave Himself for our sake
Humbled Himself to become a Servant
In our place the cross to willingly take
Is this not the Gospel, which God had sent?

Solomon is sounding candidly here that Jesus Himself is the Gospel – He is God's Good News to mankind, Gospel personified! We see Solomon the evangelist at his best in the next stanza. He responded to the challenge of evangelization and extends a call to his readers as well:

> This great salvation, which we have received
> We share with all nations and bear witness
> O this message all over be proclaimed
> And the Lord's kingdom on earth shall progress

In the last couplet Solomon proclaims that God is the greatest Giver; no one can ever outgive God:

> So the Lord God is the greatest giver
> And His name be praised now and ever!

In the sonnet on ***Joy with Children*** Solomon shares his philosophy about offspring. The phase of giving birth to children, and nurturing them - with the accompanying joys of playing with them, employing their skills, and feeling proud of them as they are growing - does not compare to anything: "More blessed than this there can be nothing"!

But later the poet acknowledges that it is not easy to supply all expected comforts or to help them to 'succeed in life achieving'. However well we may intend, the hand and help of God are inevitably essential for their fruitfulness:

> God should enable them to a worthy life
> To set a model for others to live
> And prove their chivalry in the world's strife

And to the parents a helping hand give.

A 'worthy life', being a 'model for others', proving their 'chivalry in the world's strife' and giving a 'helping hand' to aging parents – for all these, God and only 'God should enable them'! 'This we should pray for and always desire' and can aspire 'from God only'!

The last sonnet in this current section is on ***Tent on the Highest Rock***. This sonnet takes the readers with Jesus on to the Mount of Transfiguration. Like Peter on the Mount, Solomon desires to pitch his tent on the highest rock! He in fact ascended many pinnacles of achievement by his manifold art creations! And he acknowledges that his destiny was according to 'His faithful word' and that he would seek His hand and help!

The determination of the poet is vivid when he spares no cost in claiming his mountain, 'the best and noblest' designed for his 'bliss and the greatest joy'! This reminds us of Caleb in the post-patriarchal period who dared to ask, 'Give me this mountain'![31] In a similar vein, Solomon declares:

God for us sure designs the best
As He gives me a heart to seek
Although I pass the path hardest
Who can tell me that I am weak?

"Do I need an assurance still, To make it true that He's with me?" Vindicating this, the Lord enabled Solomon to stand in the pulpit to minister the Word as late as this Easter morn, in his 97th year![32]

---

31 Joshua 14:10-12
[10] And now, behold, the LORD hath kept me alive, as he said, these forty and five years … [11] As yet I am as strong this day as I was in the day that Moses sent me: as my strength was then, even so is my strength now … [12] Now therefore give me this mountain.

32 https://www.facebook.com/photo.php?fbid=10156068970163957&set=a.10150175151103957.362899.549378956&type=3&theater

B) Poems of 2013

There are a handful of poems from this time, significantly with Biblical themes and exhortations, which are dealt with at this juncture. The other poems of 2013 (namely, 'Beware Jonah', 'Camels are Coming', 'Healing Comes from God' and 'Desirable Epitaph") are dealt with later, in conjunction with related themes. Including three sonnets, which are analyzed after this section, there are 12 poems Solomon composed in 2013.

In ***The Sinner and His Song***, Solomon laments about the 'Original Sin' - the 'sin nature' inherited from Adam and exhorts about the need for watchfulness in the light of the promise of the sin-cleansing blood of the Lamb! I keep erring, he recognizes because "Old Adam's seed is in my blood". Until the day we shall reach sainthood, we have to watch our pace. What a provision and what an assurance till we reach paradise, that sinners have God's promises in His blood:

> But O, my soul, just wait in peace
> Sinners have God's promises
> In His blood He washed and keeps.

Hence as we live on earth in solace which the Lord gives, we shall 'get cure' for our disease, and our soul lives with Him. This takes us to the lines in Amy Grant's *Rock of Ages*:

> Be of sin the double cure
> Cleanse me from it's guilt and pow'r.

'The Sinner and His Song' is the title of this poem and it is its message too! Sinner being justified, and made heir of His promises, and joining the angels and the saints in the perennial and celestial song:

> Angels and saints raising the song
> Praising the Lord our God
> I shall join them and walk along
> With my Lord ever glad.

In another poem, ***The Stroke Dealt by God***, Solomon expounds the blessedness of being struck by God, in view of the outcome of finding Him through faith:

Struck deaf dumb and also darkening blind
This stroke is what our souls will truly need
So that but only through faith Him we find.

Though "Sight and speech, and touch the gift of hearing / God gave us as tools of sense perception / When God strikes a blow they disappear / And only then faith will begin action". The five senses are the gates of our perception, and we keep getting sensory thoughts constantly - some bitter some pleasant through these doors. "They go only so far and then prevent us to view the glories of heavenly shores". Only the stroke dealt by God will take us to the place where we find Him through faith.

Whereas Christ was blind to empty earth-bound glory and to pleasures and bodily pain, and was mute when He had the cross to carry the burden of our sin, "we the humans are slaves of our senses seeking blindly". We know well that "till the Lord will strike us dead in senses" we are "blind to what God wants us all to see, and deaf to what God wants us all to hear". This is very much like the strokes of an artist, which bring out hidden beauty and grandeur.

In another five-stanza poem, ***Who is He?***, Solomon discusses about Who Jesus is! He sites the many guesses about Him such as John the Baptist, Elijah, Rabbi, Scribe or Pharisee! The woman at the well could not easily tell Who He is. And Nicodemus had perceived signs and miracles He showed. How do the people see Him?

Greater than all these was He
Simon Peter once could see
By the prompting of the Lord
Him the only Son of God.

Solomon sums up his findings and declares the ultimate purpose of the Incarnation – 'to save you and me':

He was not the forerunner
But He was the true Savior
Not the chariot rider He
But came to save you and me.

In ***Redemption from Pain***, Solomon deals with the problem of pain. The universality of pain is expressed at the very outset in the first stanza:

Pain is common to all humans
Sadness is the rule of life
Crying is how life does commence
And all life's journey is a strife.

Even kings are not immune from pain and disease. Pain may be endured by means of forbearance and silence, but cannot be ended. Saints and sages have gone through this, and have set some hope for some bliss. When all is said and done, Solomon upholds the biblical truth, as enunciated by Jesus Himself, that "all pain is not God's wrath"! And ultimately, "there will be an end to suffering" - some day! "Man is not made just for weeping" the poet concludes, but to see relief some day!

In ***Waiting for a Harvest***, Solomon deals with the dynamics of harvesting! He shares a personal experience when he labored on a barren field, seeking a generous yield under the cycle of 'sowing, growing and waiting'. Since his labor was on a barren field, some thought it was 'mere waste' while others thought it a 'bad taste'. When in despair, he left the field the Lord woke him up and said that "I should not give up".

With a song in his heart he 'worked again in the same place' with the sun right in his face. The rewarding outcome is gladly recounted:

Working thus I prayed to God
To whom there is nothing hard
He sent clouds and rain along
That made the crop green and strong.

When the harvest turned out plentiful, all his barns came breaking full. And he testifies and proclaims:

I knew God will give the fruit
If I worked and afraid not.

C) Other Sonnets of 2013

We will see here three other sonnets Solomon composed as part of his early poetry as a Nonagenarian.

In ***Love and Respect***, Solomon presents a compact treatise on the twin virtues of love and respect. These are to be natural and spontaneous, springing from within and 'flowing like river'. As a 'gift from God' the bond of love must be perennial - 'blessing both receiver and the giver'! Solomon beautifully portrays this virtue in the Canaanite Ruth who had freely shown it to Naomi, and submitted her life in love. As He was pleased by this,

God in His love has firmly sealed it
A seal that lead to the Savior's advent.

Genuine love is extolled as 'God's own blessed gift'. It is 'like the blossom and its sweetest odor', which never goes adrift in the sands of time. It grows day by day and duly prospers. Solomon sums up the origin and destiny of Love in the last couplet:

Love is such that is born of God's design
So like the Divine Lily brightly shine.

The sonnet, ***Brothers Living Together***, envisages 'Brotherly Love' as enshrined in the famous passage from the Psalter (Psalm 133).[33] We see a picture of the Indian joint-family in the first stanza:

33 "Behold, how good and how pleasant *it is* for brethren to dwell together in unity."

How good for brothers to live together
Under one and the same roof as it were
If the wives do not fight with each other
And share life's blessings always together.

There are families who live with strife all the time, and there are families who live in endless harmony. Often the presence of the head of the family makes the difference! Once this authority figure is gone, there begins the strife!

The picture in the family of God with 'unity in diversity' is portrayed in the second stanza with the wonder of 'how Christ-like!':

How Christ-like to live in brotherly love
Coming from different realms whatever
Share with each other God's gifts from above
This is what a brother does to brother.

The picture of the Trinity is elucidated logically in the next stanza, with Tri + Unity – God's oneness in three persons! Elsewhere, in his reflection on one of his color woodcuts, Solomon calls this a 'heavenly arithmetic'.[34] "Thus our God has revealed His presence" and this surely is "a call to us for godly brotherhood"! This sums up the divine design, in the last couplet, for the church all through her existence on earth, until the 'rapture':

So His people live as His one body
Till they be with Him in heaven one day.

In the sonnet, ***When My Heart Went Astray***, Solomon portrays the message enshrined in the classical hymn by Purushottam Chaudhury – '*Yehova Naa Moralalinchenu*'.[35] The first two stanzas are rendering of the imagery of a wild elephant that 'has gone astray' – 'trespassing all the way'! Solomon contemplates how 'the Lord my

34 P. Solomon Raj: *St. John's Gospel*, op. cit., p. 50.

35 Andhra Christian Hymnal, Hymn No. 16.

God subdued it so kindly' – 'when my heart went astray running wildly' like the strayed wild elephant!

> He with His goad had soon controlled my heart
> Subduing my unwilling rude spirit
> And He to take hold and ever rule it
> And from me He kindly never depart.

But for God's intervention as a Mahout (the elephant rider) in his life, he could not have found the rest he enjoys now! All the cares and stress, and, snares and temptations are gone!

> O, what a rest I have now to enjoy
> And He on Him my cares always employ
> No more stress and waywardness too abroad
> And no more snares and temptations too hard.

Under this ministry of God, the poet does find 'needed safety' in His home 'And stay with Him through all eternity'!

3. Later Poetry of A Nonagenarian

A little over half of the present anthology (69 poems in all) constitutes the later poetry of Solomon as a nonagenarian. This later poetry is classified, for the convenience of the reader, into three categories – on natural themes, existential themes and Christian themes. There are some 3 sonnets and at least 3 odes in this anthology. We have seen some simple description about sonnets earlier. An ode is a kind of poem devoted to the praise of a person, animal, or thing. An *ode* is usually written in an elevated style and often expresses deep feeling. It is a poem in which a person expresses a strong feeling of love or respect for someone or something. It is otherwise described as a lyric poem of some length, usually of a serious or meditative nature and having an elevated style, and formal stanzaic structure. It is a type of lyrical stanza.

An analytical commentary on the later poetry in the above categorical scheme is in order at this juncture. There are 11 poems with natural themes, 22 poems with existential themes, and 36 poems with Christian themes. These are not, of course, watertight compartments but are a broad and ambiguous classification for the sake of dissecting this vast corpus of poetic literature. Being a Christian preacher and a theologian, Solomon's faith manifests itself in whatever category of poems we may classify, as it is embedded in every line he pens or draws.

A) Natural Themes

Let us see the poems on natural themes. The peculiar life situations and experiences recollected in these poems are interesting and entertaining – not just to the poet in his nineties but to the reader as well, whatever age group one may hail from.

There are a couple of poems in this section on 'river'. In ***The River***, Solomon graphically depicts the course of a river from the mountain pinnacles where it originates to the valley beneath: Trickle by trickle through the narrow clefts of the mountainside, hiding behind the stones and showing up again, creeping down in curvy lanes while other such small streams join it along the way. The river swiftly comes down along the mountainside, and as it reaches a sharp edge, it jumps off making a thundering sound into the gorge below - uprooting shrubs to drag them along its way, and turning around the rebellious trunks rooted firmly standing along its way; polishing the smaller pebbles, and breaking down some bigger stones; and, raising clouds of foams at last it meets the motherly belly of the deep mountain valley.

The other poem, ***Crossing the River*** also describes the course of the river in a similar streak as the above, but the last stanza here portrays a personal cruise. The river creeps, crawls and jumps in its 'native wild fury' along its way, along the mountain slopes. Crossing hurdles, turning around big bumps of boulder, leaping into the valley, and raising a cloud of mist in the process, and a rainbow in the sky above – the river flows in to slower gentle plainly land. It grows slower and wider to left and right looking like a mighty native lake. Finally it calmly tends to further slow down - slowed by the big earthen dams across, when it is easier to cross by sailboat.

The poet exuberantly depicts his cruise in the last stanza. The poet hails from the delta of the river *Godavari* in Andhra Pradesh State. *Godavari*, the largest of the peninsular rivers, has its source at Triambakam, near Nashik in Maharashtra State. It flows a length of 1465 kilometers with outfall into the Bay of Bengal, very close to the native village of Solomon Raj. Here is a cherished experience of childhood:

> Take a trip on one of the big sailboats
> Laden to the brim with dry coconuts
> Kept in course with a mighty big rudder
> Going forward with the help of the wind
> When it nearly reaches the edge
> The boatmen held it and pulled to barge

"How happy we were to have crossed the river" is the essence and the endnote.

The poem ***Childhood Memories*** describes some of the childhood memories of Solomon, which he recalls often. Not just this poem alone, though given the title, *Childhood Memories*, but most of the poems in this section are on Childhood Memories. The present incident was one of his play times with his grand mother in the rice fields of his native vicinities. Solomon calls them 'Andhra's fame'. In fact, this coastal Andhra Pradesh is acclaimed the 'rice bowl' of India – ever green with rivers, canals and water streams!

Once he was walking through the rice fields, and went ahead holding grandma's hand. Before he knew what happened, he slipped from the narrow foot-bridge into the flowing channel. Poor grandma waded into knee-deep water to save him. Save she did - to her great joy - from water! Solomon cherishes many such memories all through his life:

> Living in past memories is wonder
> Recalling events is too a game
> For some of them we go faster
> For some of them it is never the same.

In another poem, ***The Amazing Spring***, Solomon picturizes the birds and the deer, the branches and the jasmines. It was so enticing and enchanting:

> The sweetest birds do sing
> The hills response giving
> The spotted deer running
> In the sweet pleasant spring.

He describes the response of his inner being in the following stanzas: His heart was rejoicing with the swinging green branch, and his joy was surging while experiencing this memorable delight. His soul sings along with the swing of the jasmine branches, and his lower chin drops for the 'beauty of the spring'.

In the poem, ***Hatching Bird's Eggs***, Solomon vividly recollects another childhood experience. Young Solomon was "Sitting on the wooden munch / Under the shade of coconut palms" on a 'cool early dawn' in the ripe corn field. His job was to scare the stray birds because the crop was ripe. The 'open straw-bed' was rather warm. His younger sister brought for him a 'pot of cool rice water'. When she was sleeping still on the munch, and the faithful dog has gone to chase the intruding fox, Solomon decided to climb the tree nearby and hunt for birds' nests. He slowly brought one down with a few eggs to cover them up and watch hoping they hatch in another twenty days. The outcome is obvious, and well expressed in the last couple of lines:

> Bird on the tree and man on the earth
> Are always better of course.

Floating in the Air is a short poem where Solomon recounts an experience in the dream. Sometimes in dream he flies in the air. It was exhilarating as well as frustrating:

> And then I like to stay right there
> But soon I drop to earth like a stone
> And find myself on earth alone.

Flying feeling gives a strand of joy, but 'then sadness comes like a broken toy' bringing him back to where he was - "No joy, no wonder, and no bliss"!

The Toothless Smile is another poem that describes his childhood experiences. Anything can become a fit raw material for a genius, who foresees the potential therein and the end product that would transpire. The toothless smile of a baby (*bosi navvula bala*) is the content of this poem. The poet as he watches this scene about the baby, and 'the sparkling stars in her eyes', he thought that she was cute and wise. The poetic imagination sees her fists tightly closed 'as if starting to face the life-long strife', and her feet straight up 'like dancing even now taking a swing'. The poet felt so happy within for such a sweet little new life and breathed a blessing, thanking God for making her life a song.

Solomon lived and served in Vijayawada for more than a decade before leaving for overseas assignments. Again he made Vijayawada his dwelling place for nearly three decades after his retirement. Vijayawada was earlier called Bezwada, a form of Blazewada as called by the British, because of its blazing summer heat. Solomon could not but restrain himself from writing a poem on ***A Lazy Summer Afternoon***. Here, Solomon depicts the plight on a summer afternoon when time does not pass so soon:

> Wet all over the body
> With a humid kind of sweat
> Hard to sit, hard to stand
> Not so easy to understand.

No use even with two ceiling fans. They would simply go dance to send some warm air. "Getting unrobed? But to what limit? – the poet ruminates in the sweltering gloom of the hot summer afternoon.

In another poem, ***Sugarcane Plantation***, Solomon graphically portrays the interesting process of sugarcane plantation and sugar plant. The sweet smelling sight of a sugarcane field is presented in the very first stanza:

> Sweetly it smells lovely it looks
> The fertile large sugarcane field
> Rows upon rows the canes grow tall
> Till to the cutter's sickle they yield.

The process from the field to the mill starts when the farmers cut the cane and hacks dress and clean the dry leaves laying them straight in big packs and send into crushing mill wheels. At a safe distance the oven glows in big hot metal pan boiling sweet sugarcane juice thickly simmers then poured into cans for cooling. Thus goes sugar cane harvest – cut, denuded, sent to be crushed, boiled in big vats, and poured in blocks, and by this process black sugar comes. Solomon enjoyed all this with the village boys. As they loaf around there, the worker kindly cuts a piece and throws at us to chew happily.

Last couple of the poems in this section on 'Natural Themes' seems to be *odes* by an Indian poet – one on a native artifact and another on a native bird. An Ode, as seen earlier, is a kind of poem devoted to the praise of a person, animal, or thing, usually written in an elevated style often expressing deep feeling. It is a poem in which a person expresses a strong feeling of love or respect for someone or something. And Solomon, as he penned these odes, emerges as an Ode writer.

Kondapalli Wooden Man is an ode from Solomon on a native artifact from a place called Kondapalli. This woodwork is personified and Solomon wonders who ever can forget this wooden man, with hands and feet skillfully made up to scale in all detail. Forest timber and carving tools coupled with the carpenter's skill have made us dumbfound so as to fill our hearts with wonder. The eyes of the Wooden Man are like ours small and black, staring at us as we once look back, daily standing where they are kept with one's art ware. Solomon converses with it that its life is transitory as ours, made for some joy and then disappears but ultimately "contributing happiness in this world of wilderness".

Kondapalli is a small town near Vijayawada and the name is popular for its soft wood toys. They are distinct on various counts - the material being used, method of making, look and feel and themes on which these toys are made. They have been famous for many decades. Few Rajasthani *karigars* (artisans) settled over here from 16th century and started making these figures. They are referred as Aryakhastriyas.

Song to the Koel is another ode from Solomon on a native bird called *Koel.* The Asian koel is a bird of light woodland and cultivation, staying in a dense thick forest with thick trees and bamboos. It is also found in shrubby areas with tall trees, woods, villages, towns and gardens and mangrove forest. It is a shy bird, seen alone or in pair. It has straight and swift flight with rapid wing beats. It is an omnivorous bird, feeding mainly on fruits and berries, feasting on the ripe fruits, and also feeding on insects, eggs, small vertebrates and caterpillars. Asian Koel is very vocal. It is often heard before seen: song of the male is a repeated *koo-Ooo- koo-Ooo- koo-Ooo*. The female makes a shrill *kik-kik-kik*… call.[36]

Solomon welcomes the dear *koel*, perched on the green mango tree. He personifies this native bird and declares that "nothing in the world stops your singing" the joyful spring song to us, humans - even dreadful winter rain, or the blowing eastern wind. He welcomes the *koel*, coming from the freezing north, to stay with us as long as she wants. The melody of her song is sweet and the music of her sweet song "Redeems us from sadness" and the poet praises the little *koel* as 'conqueror of misery'. Finally, the poet invites her again after her departure for the current season:

> When you leave us here dear *koel*
> You come to see us once again
> To feed us with your sweet song
> And to relieve us from our woes.

B) Existential Themes

Having seen the poems with natural themes, it is time for visiting his 22 poems with existential themes, such as social evils, trials and troubles, solitude and companionship and his sunset years. Let us see the seven poems on **social evils**, which are short but straightforward:

Black Coffee is a small poem in which Solomon addresses the prejudices and predilections about 'black coffee' – which is becoming a global familiarity of our times. Though, he dreams of black coffee in the bed after being well-fed, he hates to see it the morning for reasons not stated. It could be because of a forced wake-up too early than normal, or it could be because of its imperfect proportion of the components. Though others may like to drink, thinking that it keeps them awake from sleep, and relishing its bitter taste, he personally thinks that 'it is all a waste'.

Houses to Live is another short poem where Solomon addresses the social evils of injustice and 'unjust distribution of wealth'. Indeed, "a house to live is gift of God"! This some of us receive while some have no place to live. We do not know the reason why? While some

36 https://en.wikipedia.org/wiki/Asian_koel.

command spacious palaces, some do not even have a hut. Anyway, Solomon proclaims that poverty is the child of injustice, though it is not poor man's fault! "Unjust distribution of wealth does make some people poor"! And complaints, sit outs, and agitations cannot provide the cure.

In another poem, ***Wealth to Show Mercy***, Solomon evolves a new hermeneutic to offset the above evil. The biblical basis for this is the story of the poor leper and the rich man, who both died – but the former went the 'blissful side' while 'not so the other one'. The 'why' of it was answered in the lines:

> We may ask why it was so
> One was patient in his faith
> The other did only know
> To drown deep in worldly wealth.

When all is said and done, the summary envisages that wealth, besides other things, is given 'for us to show mercy'! Poor humans forget this, but at the end when they try to see, 'the door then shall be shut'.

The short poem, ***The Bazar***, is just a narrative of a typical Indian *bazar* (market). You see 'crowds moving all around' the city roads in the dusty wind - shopping, loafing, sightseeing, even some lazy walking. How much more? It seems unending to walk around in the city dusty bazar, walking on the melting coal tar.

Meetings and Conferences is another short poem that depicts the routine of 'meetings, consultations, conferences and agendas, chairmen, presidents, welcomes and farewells'. The procedural norm is stated that 'everything' is to be done openly, collectively, democratically and sometimes ecumenically. 'Democratic discussions - Never one man's decision'! Though we hold on to this norm, the poet laments that 'at the end, that happens as one man's way'.

The poem on ***TV Preachers*** presents the sad state of affairs with "Many anxious TV preachers now". The poet laments how they make him tired of the Gospel, which he loves:

> They try to impress me with loud noise
> What can be told in gentle voice.

In another beautiful stanza he elucidates their sad plight:

> Throat is their tool and volume their trick
> Hoping the listener changed and quick
> But seldom have they a tool to measure
> How much the listeners got of the treasure.

The Gospel in fact is simple but we try to make it heavy, trying to feed the lambs with meat while they only need milk. And to everyone's dismay, "Meat instead of milk makes the poor lambs sick". Having been a preacher all his life, Solomon aptly points out:

> Preachers seldom have learnt the skill
> Of teaching people with more good will
> Using our Lord's beautiful fare
> Of flowers o' the field and the birds o' the air.

Solomon's last poem on social evils, ***Human Wild Beasts***, strongly condemns tragic crimes like rape. Enraged in his spirit probably by the 2012 Delhi Gang Rape case, the poet pens his strong feelings and convictions addressing the inhuman evils in a civilized society.

Man becomes inhuman sometimes, committing tragic crimes. It is hard to see and hard to overcome the shock and shame it brings. "Some youth today have lost their soul and forfeited their shame, making all our poor conscience foul and bringing to us bad name". The poet bemoans "Rape and kill a poor virgin - In a fast moving bus: How sad and painful to imagine, and how greatly disastrous!"

We feel the pain deep in our heart and now believe that "man is much worse than the beast" which lives in the wilderness. "A blooming life nipped in the bud, and a story told all the same"! Our conscience can never stop grieving in agony and shame!

Then, there are four poems Solomon wrote about **trials and troubles**. In the sonnet, ***Troubles Come Together***, Solomon portrays the glorious purpose of troubles in one's life. He describes how 'troubles come together and not alone'. He likens them to the herd of camels from father Abraham's house, as Eliezer was sent in search of a bride for Isaac. A great illustration with a message is presented here. If only we show kindness and love to the camels, they take us home to the bridal palace. The noble purpose for which the Father sends the camels (troubles) is for us to get abundant solace, and "to be received with great royal acclaim!"

Solomon sums up the message in the last stanza and the couplet. This is surely great and good news to our life to face problems when they come together, to be prepared to face our own strife, and to ever win Satan in His name:

Defeat the foe with the sign of the cross
And inherit the great kingdom at last.

Camels are Coming is another poem with a similar message as above. When "Camels come in a long big row, we do not chase them away" but 'give them water' and show mercy, because "To God's home they know the way". Camels imply troubles, and they are from the father's yard. "He sends them to bring the bride, so that she comes happy homeward, and to his son be wedded".

Solomon enlightens the reader that "trials and pains are the camels", and if we "treat them well with cool water" and "put on them the proper saddle", they will surely take you to the father. What you sow you reap, always even more! This is true of the scriptural law of giving. This is beautifully portrayed by Solomon in the following stanza:

In return to the food to the camels
Get gold bangles to your hands
And to the others in the house
There are gifts too and garlands.

Figuratively Solomon presents the three Persons of the Godhead - the Father and the Son (who is the bridegroom) and the Holy Spirit (who is the Guide). Assuredly, trials like camels show us the way - the right path to the bride-groom's feet!

The poem ***As the Wind Blows*** presents a simple and sound teaching on the Holy Spirit and His ministry to the believer. Solomon exhorts himself ('my soul') to follow the Lord's leading. The Spirit shows silently as the wind blows gently. Jesus likened the Spirit to the wind and this metaphor is aptly used here. If we keep proceeding in the Lord's path, the poet assures:

> You will not falter in your step
> Your goal you will not give up.

As He sends His angels to keep you from dangers, and brings us to His home guiding, we need to lean upon His bosom believing, when perils do appear and sadness comes near. He is able and kind hearted; He knows where we started, and He will make all our path straightened.

God's Ways are Greater is another poem related to the theme of trials. In this, the poet exhorts us not to fret when things go wrong, and when there's no song in our mouth. God knows what is good for us and His plans are always great and true. When we show great desire to the earthly kingdoms, we do not see God's kingdom since our eyes are blinded.

When Jesus died on the cross His friends thought it was a loss. Desolate they went again to fishing, their old bargain. Jesus then opened their eyes and showed them that His rule will rise. Blessed are they who perceive and receive His promises!

Then, there are four poems on **solitude and companionship.** They bring out the individual benefits of both solitude and companionship maintaining a desirable equilibrium. The first poem, ***Blessedness of Loneliness***, is a five stanza Ode on Loneliness. Human beings crave for the twin gifts of company and communication. Without company they feel vulnerable. Surely, the gift of speech, which facilitates communication, is also a great gift to mankind. But we desire both of these only in small measure. Evil company can lead to tears and sharp tongue can burn like wild fire. They both appear harmless but soon the fun will disappear.

Hence, Solomon advocates that one should sit silently sometimes, trying to hear the still small voice. This we can hear only quietly 'since we become deaf with noise'! Further, our souls do get richly sustained in waiting for God's presence, and the holy countenance of God can be seen only in the lonely places.

Companionship is another short poem, which extols the blessedness of communion and companionship. Human heart craves for company. Loneliness is vulnerable just as nature abhors vacuum. Solomon extols the blessedness of the gift of speech. Speech is the greatest gift to humans to communicate. A silent person is either dumb, or he is 'a sage in forest in silence'. We are told that God the Father is always in communion with the Son and the Holy Spirit, as the doctrine of Trinity envisages. Solomon describes this beautifully elsewhere: 'One God and three persons / A symbol of perpetual unity'.[37]

It is aptly pointed out that 'no man is an island', and the gregarious instinct in man propels him to communion and community. Solomon portrays this universal need in the poem, ***Man is Not Made to be Alone***. Solomon beautifully picturizes the foolishness of denouncing friendship but only to remorse:

In blundering selfish pride
Like a wildest horse I ride
And called my friend a fool and then in remorse I wept.

The friend denounced thus did not say a word in response but this sears the poet sharply through his heart like a bitter sword. Learning lessons from his foolish past, the poet in a friendly way shared his love with a stranger lad in a cool and kindly mood, which made him really glad. From this experience, and from the supreme example of Jesus Christ, comes the enlightenment that humans are not made or meant to be alone:

Humans are not made alone
In lonely burdens to only groan
The good Lord made them to each other's concerns make known.

Jesus, Our Savior and Lord came here to bear our woes and give His life as a ransom for all our sins on the cross.

---

37 *St, John's Gospel*, op. cit., p. 50.

In the last poem in this section, ***Then and Now***, Solomon proposes the need for icebreakers for friendship.

I did not know your name
But often I saw you going this way
Once I tried to stop you and ask the same
So as to be your friend every day.

Now that I know your name
And since I became your friend
Life now is no longer the same
We shall be friends till the end.

Finally, there are seven poems on his **sunset years**. The first poem, with the title ***End of the Journey***, is a Sonnet. It is not the first time for Solomon to contemplate and write on the 'end of the journey'. His anthology of hymns, *Geetha Malika* contains many lyrics on this recurring theme. Also in his Songs from Sambalikan, we find this theme. In the present sonnet, Solomon supplicates to the Lord, as now his journey comes to an end. The ravages of time are expressed in the words, 'bruised and wounded' and 'sores and cuts'. Only the Lord can mend them as he comes to His door and His gate 'greatly renowned'.

Solomon recollects the divine call in the prime of his life. The Lord asked him to go to work in His vineyard 'with tools and wares', and he obeyed the call never counting the cost, and the Lord has taken on Him all his cares. Having been impacted by the teaching of St. Francis of Assisi, Solomon acknowledges what he was enabled to do in the course of his ministry:

When there was sadness I tried to sow joy
And where there was strife I tried to bring peace
Where there was greed there real contentedness
Which *mantra* St. Francis too did employ.

Even when he did not get commendation from people, he went ahead and labored all the same.

Desirable Epitaph is another poem Solomon wrote in 2013 related to the sunset years. This seven stanza poem has a numerical significance. As seven denotes completeness or perfection, the exhortation and the enlightenment the poet envisages in each of the poem is edifying. He addresses this poem to an anonymous friend declaring, 'life is too short'. We make the best of it as we work hard in the given task, and show now our stewardship skills. Secondly, a great life lived and a high virtue only will last and be of great worth, but not riches, lands, or great wealth that we leave on earth when we die. Thirdly, he exhorts not to 'fall in sloth and slumber' as it will make life a waste. Some have failed to remember this and therefore left nothing of any good taste. Fourthly, the poet exhorts never to stop acquiring wisdom, as it helps to charter our path and keeps us from sad fall - saving us from nature's wild wrath. Fifthly, as we make friends in life we are to do it wisely. For, evil friendships are a pest, and they can bring us great misery - leading life to big unrest. Sixthly, we see the exhortation not to be a lender or a debtor, but to live within our means, be thrifty and share our cup with the poor. There is an allusion in this stanza to Shakespeare's *Hamlet*, where Polonius counsels his hotheaded son Laertes:

> Neither a borrower nor a lender be,
> For loan oft loses both itself and friend,
> And borrowing dulls the edge of husbandry.[38]

Finally, the poet assures his friend to go in peace when the call comes, as he will see his reward in God, and the life he has lived in grace will be engraved on his epitaph.

The three-stanza poem on ***Miracles*** presents a three-fold message envisaging the salient insights from Solomon's pen: First, the poet says that he does "not seek a miracle to showing to men what God can do". For, miracle for miracle's sake doesn't aid building up of

38 (Act-I, Scene-III, Lines 75-77), https://literarydevices.net/neither-a-borrower-nor-a-lender-be/.

faith; it is just like a crutch. Standing on faith is required for stability and growth:

> He who wants a miracle crutch
> Does not stand on his faith as such.

Secondly, being content with miracles to the neglect of fulfilling His commands amounts to folly. 'Faith based on miracles does not stand' just 'Like a man builds his house on sand'. Finally, the injunction as given by Jesus is to 'not rejoice that you can do miracles' as 'they will not benefit you'. Rather, we need to rejoice that our name is rightly written in the Book of Life.

The Call and The Journey portrays the mystery and the miracle of the Call of God and the ensuing Journey. The five stanzas are like ascents in the journey. This is obviously Solomon's testimony about the blessedness of obeying the Call of God. This is like a Psalm of Ascents in the Hebrew Scriptures:

"When He said to me "come"/ I didn't know what I get"
– the poet confesses.
"But when I simply went to Him / What I saw was perfect"
– No regrets!
"He wanted me to leave / some comforts of my own"
– a step in self-denial.
"But what great blessings He could give/To me till then unknown"
– divine surprises!
"Great wine and living bread / More than I ever see"
– amazing supply.
"He kept in store to keep me fed / And make me rested"
– divine provision!
"Fellowship of great lords / And company of saints"
– awesome communion.
"I did get as I went forwards / And royal rich garments"
– robes of righteousness!
"My mouth was filled with song / Right along all the way"
– perennial melodies.
"And I had strength right in my wing / To reach the clouds and stay"
– rapture!

Offerings is another five-stanza poem giving us his ruminations of the sunset years. These are six-line stanzas. When all the labors of life have ended Solomon reckons that he spent his life with the Lord thankfully. And as the time of rest becomes immanent to him, he calls upon Him to come and help. So he forgets all that belongs to self and peacefully waits to see His face.

In the second stanza, as one enters the next destination, Solomon depicts the blessedness and the reward. We have 'no need for any worldly lust' as all our needs in Him are fully met when we reach our heavenly rest. What a reward is the whitest stone the Lord will give, with a name known only to those that receive! This we will never get in our strength alone!

In the third stanza, Solomon describes how all the promises we have lived to see are coming to be fulfilled now for us - since the Lord has always been faithful! Then we begin to see in full the glory in which He ever lives, and the everlasting peace He alone gives.

The poet has seen along the way some flowers and also thorns, which signify several praises and a few scorns. He tried to bear the both with His help and His grace was enough for him to live. He testifies of the peace which only He can give, while adding blessing upon blessing.

Finally, he yields himself to the Lord in gratitude for His grace, which is 'wider than all my strife', and His love, which is 'still greater all through my life':

That which I did and what I couldn't do
I remit humbly all, my Lord, to you
And ask you to fulfill this for me …
And now I come forever your face to see.

Old Age Comes presents a beautiful description of old age and the practical counsel for this particular season of life. Solomon accepts the divine plan for man's existence and exit from life. Solomon hurrays old age, as it has come at last. In this state of life there won't be any 'hustle bustle' as 'You do not run now so fast'. A new life style is ushered as you wake up at night once or twice, with late mornings. A new etiquette is in place as you 'take your time at the dining place', 'chew and swallow', as 'it is not a race'. It is no longer time to 'crack hard nuts' lest 'your dentures break in bits'. Let your food be soft and spicy and 'This is wise as you would see'!

And it's more pleasant to talk along: 'Do not sit and keep silent' is the rule of the time and space. Further, a new trend of conversation with eagerness to share and share, as if it's their 'endless vocation':

Wisdom is what you like to share
Even if others do not always care
Where should your experience go
If you to others do not show.

It is, of course, fair that our experience should not go in vain, but be shared and cherished! But a word of caution - not to welcome verbal duel, as it is a 'sure fuel to bitterness'! "Learn to say, Yes - always / Whatever the opponent says"!

Finally, the whole counsel in fact is Solomon's soliloquy – speaking to himself and others too in the process! He sums up his counsel in the last stanza:

Look ahead to a peaceful end
People bid farewell and send
For a while if they remember you
Know it as an added blessing too.

To Be With My Lord is the last poem in this section, which expresses the 'blessed assurance' Solomon has, as a result of the life-long revelation he has received, and believed. In a similar vein, as the 19th century poet, Sarah Flower Adams penned it in the hymn, "Nearer, my God, to Thee", Solomon expresses his desire to be with his dear Lord, 'good shepherd and a sure guide':

My desire is to be with my dear Lord
He is my good shepherd and a sure guide
I have his great promise and good firm word
Which long ago in his presence I heard.

I shall steadfastly swim holding his hand
To cross the deep dark river and be safe

And surly reach my father's holy land
Where there is no more hard labor and grief.

Singing songs in praise to God, I live there
Always, angelic hosts with me to be
In perfect bliss and joy for ever share
This is what the Lord had promised to me.

C) Christian Themes

The remaining 36 poems with Christian themes are the cream of the collection dealing with manifold items like Praise and Worship (2), Biblical Characters (4), Waiting upon the Lord and Healing (3), Shepherd (3), Liturgy (5) and other miscellaneous themes (19).

There are a couple of poems on **praise and worship**. In ***Adoration*** worship to the Creator God is invoked. We sing praises profusely, and offer our worship to God our Lord. He created the heaven and the earth and the depths of the space, just by His Word. His name is holy and worthy of praise. Heaven and earth and the whole creation shall raise songs to him and adore him in faith forever. Reigning above and watching all creation, He receives praises of heavenly hosts. Responding to him in adoration and declaring his might for ever:

Worthy is the creator and our God
Worthy to be adored and be worshipped
Who keeps us safe by his staff and his rod
We declare his might with voices equipped.

How to Worship You My Lord? is another poem on praise and worship. The poet engages in a dialogue with God, in an intimate 'I-Thou' relationship. 'How to worship you my Lord?' – he asks, and how to 'adore your lotus feet'? And, How to get His kindly word, comforting and sweet? There is a metaphor here where God's feet are called 'lotus feet'!

The poet wonders what is pleasing to His heart as a gift from him to God, and with what offering he should start, and what is it that He wants from him? It is strange He never asks gold and silver or incense, and He never makes our task burdensome. The poet offers repentance and tearful heart, and reconciliation to His feet and pleads for confirming forgiveness.

Again the poet wonders what offering He wants most. He feels that a willing heart and a loving soul are pleasing to His taste and that He never calls more than these! He feels it strange that God never asks a gift. Since he is a pauper, he believes that He surely lifts fallen souls to give praise and honor Him!

He recollects his role models from historical and biblical accounts at this juncture: His servant Holy Francis (of Assisi) discarded his mantle robe, walked shoe-less with gunny robe and went to preach in sack raiment. And, a poor woman seeking grace and forgiveness washed His feet with her tears of deep disgrace and poured perfume as an adoring treat. *Bhakthi* is what the Lord seeks, he raises these as gifts to Him: an ear to hear and a mouth to praise, and seeking to walk in His path.

Then, we see four poems on three of the **biblical characters** – Jonah from the Old Testament, Thomas from the New Testament and an anonymous woman popularly known as the Samaritan woman or the woman at the well. It is interesting to see that this woman and her story are Solomon's favorite raw material for his art as well as for his verse. It is well known that his famous dance drama, *Kim Kartavyam* was woven around her story.

Beware Jonah is a poem from 2013 depicting the eternal message that God cares when people perish. The poet elucidates the blessing of doing 'the task that the Lord has assigned to you' – here, "to take a ship going to Nineveh shore to call people to repent, turn to God". When He sent you to Nineveh, but if you ignore that job and take a ship to safe Tarshish, then God sends a whale to swallow you and bring you back to tell the Ninevites so men and all creatures return to God, and know how God cares for the people when they perish. Apart from a narrative, the poem is didactic, enlightening people of the ways of God!

Doubting Thomas as he was commonly called, was not an agnostic, but a saint and a great martyr, as we know him. We poor humans always ask questions and experiential proofs. No one suspects sunrise or sunset, since we see them happen always with us, but rising from death no one really expects. In fact, only Jesus did rise again from death.

Thomas wanted to see by sight, which in a way is quite unwise. For knowledge of God comes only through faith, and we will never need wisdom for that. So Thomas the doubtful never counted it a loss to ask visual proof to see Him. Ultimately, Thomas, who was one of the apostles, himself died for Christ on Thomas Mount.

There are two poems on the woman at the well in this collection. ***Women At the Well!*** is a sonnet, where the poet addresses the woman at the 'solitary well' in the Samaritan village. He engages her in a conversation asking about the thoughts in her heart and anxious soul as she came along the way with empty pot seeking water from Jacob's blessed well. He asks her if she is not content with the places to worship their creator and God, even the great Gerizim their holiest mount, and the kings and the great realms.

The poet welcomes her to meet Jesus who comes that day there to her, and assures her that He can give her what she seeks - freedom from hunger and liberty - and that He will surely break all barriers. He wishes that He may be her great savior today, whom she knows as great Messiah.

In the other poem, ***O Woman at the Well***, the poet employs the conversational mode and talks with the woman at the well, who was standing alone and looking around. He asks whether she is looking for 'blessed commemoration of ancestors and their gifts' or searching to visit pilgrim centers. He clarifies to her that though she may have all these one-day, but still she is lost. He gently focuses on what she needs most and leads her to Jesus Who will give what she asks:

> Better know what you need and ask for it
> Better know what it is that you need most
> And know who He is now speaking to you
> And ask Him He will give.

We see three poems now on **Waiting upon the Lord and Healing.** In the five stanzas of the poem, ***Waiting Upon the Lord***, Solomon distinguishes between praying and waiting.

When he prayed before his God he confesses that he talked all the time, not He - asking Him for all he needs, but He has given all to him. So he resolves:

Therefore let me wait on Him
In silence to what He says.

He often prayed and asked the Lord so he try and help himself. So far he is well and good; when he needs he asks for help. So now he resolves:

If I waited on the Lord
He will do what I cannot.

He often tried to tell the Lord knowing not what He can give; he asked for petty things he needs, but He can give so much more. Therefore, he resolves now:

So let me now wait on Him
For He gives more glorious gifts.

He did not tell Him in prayer that he wants to serve Him now; and that he will do His will for His sake, if He kindly shows him how. So now he resolves:

I pray and wait on the Lord
Till He calls and lets me serve.

If now he waits on the Lord, he shall get his health renewed like an eagle flies upward - running and never tired. So finally he resolves:

Walking fast I shall not fall
He shall leave me not at all.

There are two poems on healing and health. ***Healing Comes from God*** is a poem from 2013. A couple of insights are elucidated by means of participant observation (method of research) in this short poem. The poet sat with people in sickness, and in deep and acute pain. Some wept and wailed in deep distress while others simply moan. The poet observes that it is the sign of a weak heart to go over all misfortunes and cry in many words; It makes pain all the more worse. Medicine helps to make pain less and doctors have some cures. The essential message of divine healing is summed up in the last two lines:

> In spite of all our loud complaints
> Only God our health restores!

The other poem is like a treatise or a discourse on ***Sickness and Health***. Several truths are lucidly presented in this long poem, which shine forth as *nav ratan* (nine jewels) of healing and health:

1) Mortal body is made of clay breakable on any day, brittle and fragile just like a mud-made pot and shredded one day on the spot.
2) Though kept lovingly with all great care and nourished with good fare all the time, no one knows why it gets so sick and receives the painful prick, when it gets into such a bitter state. It was once so sweet though, when it was quite healthy and hale riding joyful clouds and sail.
3) As we all know, sickness strikes both the rich and the poor alike - sometimes lasting long and deep, and sometimes making shorter sweep.
4) Often we do not know what brings torment to our healthy wings, whether it is wind and rain or summer shine, or even dirt and unclean food.
5) Man had fought with sickness too long, when medical skill was not strong. Plagues and pestilences wiped the earth with coffins carried or bodies burnt. Men fled from the plague migrating, as solution to the problem looked vague. Men worshipped the trees and the brooks, giving floral homage, but looked helpless.
6) Sinfulness too is said to be the cause of sickness as we see: Forgiveness will restore the health and brings back healing wealth.
7) Forgiveness and prayer heal when sickness was coming on sinful wheels. God who tests our faith through pain brings us wholeness once again.

8) In the light of all the above, don't blame others when sickness comes. God wills our good always. Wisdom tells that if we bear the pain God will make us whole again.
9) Silence and some forbearance sure can cure with God-given herbs; But when God's time has come to go we should be prepared also.

Then we see three poems on the theme of a shepherd. First of all, there is a seven-stanza poem with the title, ***You Shepherds***, written as a seven-fold call to the shepherds of the Lord's flock.

The first stanza is like a wakening call to the godly shepherds to be awakened, never once to cast their eyelid as their flock is out grazing, and the wolf is hiding behind the fence.

In the second stanza the poet calls the shepherds to wear their staff and their rod in hand to protect their sheep always; to keep them safe from disastrous land; and to lead them through the safest ways.

The third stanza exhorts the shepherds to walk their sheep to the cool fountain springs so that they drink their fill and feel refreshed. Thus they heed to their kind biddings and never feel distressed.

The fourth stanza urges never to leave the weakling lamb but to take it on their strong shoulder; preventing strain to its body and giving it a new song.

The fifth stanza encourages the shepherds to stand by the sheep when danger comes near and to give their life as their owner. But the bondsman runs away seeing the wolf to save his life.

The sixth stanza calls forth the shepherds to gather the sheep together safe into the warm shelter, when the evening shadows fall. After all, they know their voice and their calling.

The last stanza points to the way of Lord Jesus Christ, the Chief Shepherd, who wants us to follow Him and serve Him, as we have listened to His voice.

There is another short poem on ***The Shepherd*** giving simple but relevant instructions. A shepherd, while keeping little sheep, first of all, must give green grass to his herd and take them to shade to sleep. He must then hold fast his staff and rod to draw the straying sheep, to drive the wolf abroad, and to keep the flock safely. Again, he must walk before the sheep to call them by quiet call and lead all of them till they reach the safe stall. This is what Lord Jesus, the prime Shepherd has told and did for us - so we reach His household.

A Pastor's Duties is the last poem on this theme. A five-fold exhortation, related to Pastor's duties, is given in the five stanzas of this poem. As shepherds of the souls pastors have to do it carefully in intent, for, this vocation involves fruits that shine in the firmament.

Apart from pastoral care, personal care is emphasized. Here is a great advise from the poet who has been a pastor to all the pastors:

Do a good reading of the Word
Never assume you know it all
The more you spend your time with God
The more power your sermon call.

Then, pastors are exhorted to pray for their people everyday so that the Spirit prepares them well. As a result, their hearts will look for Sunday, and the pastor's harvest will be full.

Then, the holy obligation to rebuke and set men right for God's sake is stressed. God forgives the poor soul that errs, but never forsakes any soul. He offers His abundant mercy.

Finally, pastors are exhorted to give respect to all their colleagues, as they need their prayers in their task. A saintly man believes this and will ask for this gift from God.

There are some five poems on **Liturgy, Church, Faith of Our Fathers,** and **the Wonder of His Calling.**

The poem on ***Liturgy*** is a sonnet where Solomon extols liturgy, its parts and blessings. In a way, we consider this as a didactic sonnet for its educational value. Liturgy is a wondrous gift to the Church; it is in fact God's great gift to divine worship - helping us to lift our hearts heavenwards and to sing and praise God with others' fellowship.

What a great privilege to us is Invocation, calling the worshipper to heed God's Word. Then we have Confession and Absolution (pardon or forgiveness), which we need. It is a great bliss guiding us in worship. Then, end the worship with Blessing from altar or Benediction. Step by step we are guided in the act - with the angels and saints from near and far, as our hearts start the heavenly journey. The last couplet sums up the design and the destiny of liturgy:

Liturgy indeed is a part of our life
Nourishing our souls to eternal life.

The poem on ***The Church*** is enlightening, with the meaning and nature of the Church well portrayed. What the Church is and what it is not are elucidated:

The church is not a building
However big and beautiful it be
The Church is a place with people living
A 'church-like' life for others to see.

The Church is not a place to seek glory, honor and the foremost seat. But our Lord had really taught servant-hood and a meek life.

The Church is not meant to announce our great works of righteousness like the old Pharisee did once foolishly - telling God much of his godliness.

The church is a place to get free and abundant forgiveness by God's grace, remission for all our sins, and then to be counted in His holy race. The publican who had cast down his head in remorse and shame knew that he was indeed forgiven. So, we should all do.

The church is for worship and praise, thanking God for all that He gave and to raise our both hands to Him - imploring Him to kindly save.

There are a couple of poems in a series on the **faith of our fathers.** The first poem, ***Faith of Our Fathers-1*** declares the heritage and proclaims the present resolve in five different situations, as found in the five stanzas. The Faith of our Fathers is great and mighty, the poet declares. And the resolve, first of all, is to fight with Satan, and to give witness to the Lord's Name as long as we live in the world.

The resolve in the midst of four other different situations is expressed in the following stanzas as given below:

When we are hungry and be poor, we care for the man next-door, robe the naked to cover his shame and comfort him in Jesus' Name.

When the rich oppress us, we want to bear such patiently. And when in the world we have no name, we have the Name of Christ.

When we are denied all comfort, we take resort with the faithful, living outside the village bounds but hearing always the heavenly sounds.

We are not sad for all we missed, for reward was promised to us. All that we see is a bubble, but we have a heritage stable.

The second poem, ***Faith of Our Fathers-2***, presents the need for His continuing help in the midst of different challenges. There is the same refrain at the end of each of the four stanzas:

Faith of our Fathers guiding us
Help us to be true to Thee.

As we pass in the sinful world, and as we see darkness all around; When we were hungry and poor, He has taught us to show mercy, and, when we call the helpless to our door, to give them a morsel taking pity.

Our ancestors were unlettered, counting on fingers of their hand, and, losing their lands for loans battered, without a shelter to sit or stand.

Faith of our Fathers, hope, and trust kept us alive through all the strife; Bearing the cross in patience, we must go on seeking a better life:

Faith of our Fathers guiding us
Help us to be true to Thee.

When He Called is a short poem that portrays the wonder of His calling! It seems to be the personal testimony of the poet, as well as the experience of many who have responded to His call unconditionally. Four essentials of this calling are described in the four stanzas respectively. First of all, he could not see why, when He called him to come, but when he simply went to Him he did not need to try the reason. Then, when He wanted me to leave some comforts of his own, he did not know that He could give more than the world had shown. Again, He kept on board much ahead - the richest wine and ample bread better than I ever seen, even Manna from high heaven. Further, the nearness of the Lord and the fellowship of the saints was his share and he could go forward with the blessed sacraments.

Finally, there remain some 19 poems of Solomon, from his Later Poetry as Nonagenarian. These are all on different miscellaneous themes.

You Give Darshan Before I Seek is a short poem that reminds us of the prophecy from Isaiah.[39] The poet wonders how the Lord is already there even before he sits to pray, waiting for him and clearly says that He is not so far away. Again, before some words come to his tongue the poet hears His soothing words clearly and sees all the comfort He brings and rejoices in the words he hears.

Whereas the poet just seeks Him with some desire in feeble faith and lingering doubt, His countenance burns his heart like sure fire and fear goes out. 'How can I have some doubts again?' – the poet declares when His love to him is so clear. As he clearly hears His voice, the poet gets assurance.

The poem, ***Second Plan***, enlightens the reader on God's second chance when we fail or when we lose the given opportunity. There is always a second chance with God. And second plan God shows us isn't bad if we see it like God sees it. May be we were glad in the first plan, but the second can prove better. When we accept it without murmur, we then can see the wonder.

The poet exhorts not to seek always the good old place if it is not God's desire for us. Should we aspire for Bithynia comforts and its solace? If we want to do God's will, we shall ask His guidance and be still.

Go to Troas and wait and stand, and God sends someone with a plea to bring the Gospel to Western land. That is God's plan for you. Even if it is a second offer for you, take it up and you will prosper.

When all is said and done, the second offer will not be bad; In fact, it will be more blessed. If you accept it, you will not be sad; for,

39 Isaiah 65:1 "I revealed myself to those who did not ask for me; I was found by those who did not seek me".

it is what God wanted for you. Therefore you see that the second offer will exceed in excellence in God's providence.

A Fool's Prayer is another poem with didactic message. A fool may pray hours long but it goes only roof high. A broken clock will make a big decoration but its cry will be dumb. From this the lesson is drawn that a still small cry, or a repentant moan sounds louder than you hear, but it reaches inner parts of heaven where the Father will surely hear. God looks for man's inner mind and hears his repentant cry. And those who seek His mercy will find and will get reply surely.

The Story of the Ladder is a short poem communicating couple of lessons. You don't need a ladder to climb the hedge-high bush because you are taller to step on it and easily crush. The two lessons we have are clear, if we really want to discern: One is that you are greater than the bush with heart and soul to seek your God and follow Him as He would wish for us. And the other lesson is that "if there is a will there is a way".

Ears to Hear is another short poem that is an eye opener for one and all. The wisest man can get it wrong some times when he reads the scripture. The certain way to get it right and to get all the needed guidance is to seek the help of the Holy Spirit. Strangely sometimes we get the message, but it is not always so.

'He that has ears to hear' the meaning that the Spirit gives will never make it wrong. There are some symbols in the Holy Writings that need to be discerned. And the Spirit, if we seek, will surely lead us into Truth.

What Do We Seek? is a six-stanza poem presenting different people seeking different things from Jesus! There are a handful of accounts of the Gospel narrative. First, the woman with issue of blood touched His garment's end lightly. She did not ask any worldly good but wanted her sickness to end. Secondly, the man at the temple born blind did not know what he should have asked, but went as told to the pool to find a wonder and his received sight. Thirdly, the paralytic at the pool who lied there for several years obeyed Christ's call carefully and his disease disappeared. Then, Jairus came to ask nothing but new life for his daughter who died. Jesus kindly granted him that and Jairus was satisfied. Finally, the good Roman centurion did not think he was truly good but asked Christ to just heal his man and Christ the merciful did. All these people only wished to get health and healing, but they did not seek loaves and fish, which we may easily forget.

Seeing and Hearing is a short poem pointing to a picture that is hanging on the wall, to solicit all that it makes us recall. The problem of pain, an age-old problem is addressed in this poem with philosophical musings:

> Is it that made all the kingdoms fade?
> Or is it that made all oceans dry
> Or what made the heavens brightly awake
> Is it the fiery devil that can evil make?
>
> What is it that keeps the wall from fall?

All the red bricks, all the water, cement and mortar - Do they keep it without falling forever? What can ensure its permanency in the midst of threatening wind, rain and storm? This is the song of human pain - the eye to see and the ear to hear! Rocks do not have any of these and they cannot hear or see.

The short poem on ***Daily Prayer*** is a panegyric on prayer! The daily prayer is like milk for us to nourish the inner man. So we never fret to sit in prayer but sit and talk to God at length. In prayer we sit with Christ side by side and drink deep His love and the bliss. We ride on the big cloud of Jesus' love till we touch the glorious hem of heaven.

We see the countenance of the blessed Lord and rejoice to hear His loving voice. Our soul responds willingly to His word making us completely deaf to this world. What a joy to sit silent and pray, and cast away all our cares and concerns. Prayer time is a blessed time, and we will rejoice if we sit in prayer day by day.

Song of A Little Lamp is a short poem with five little stanzas. 'Let me shine and show the way!' – has been the heart-cry of Solomon all through his ministry years! He wrote a lyric in 1970's on this theme, *Naaloni Premajyotini Velunganeeyumaa* - which was a 'hit' of all times. Again when he rendered into English the 44 lyrics from his *Gaana Kusumaalu*, which were broadcast on radio, *Voice of the*

Gospel after over three decades, it was published as *Geetha Malika.* Apart from translating this song like all others, he gave two more alternative renderings for this particular lyric – expressing his heart's desire in different words. This is echoed again now in this poem, even in his nineties!

In roaring darkness, raging wind, to stand and show His light the Lord has kept me firm to stand and to declare His might. The stormy winds do rise and rage, but they 'cannot quench me', the poet says. His purpose is so strong and wise and His plans endure forever. The wayfarer and one long lost will find his path again and reach the safe haven at last when he forgets all the pain. Sinners who have gone astray will see his light to find the way and cast away all fears and succeed. Hence the resolve:

So let me shine and show the way
To those who need the light
Till at the end they all may stay
In peace, forget the fright.

Pilgrims is another short poem, in which the poet portrays the blessedness of the pilgrims to the Holy Land. Blessed are the pilgrims who hold some relics in their hand, with memories with us for a long time. The poet fondly remembers great places like holy Constantinople, holy sites the saints have walked in the past, and places lived by many faithful people.

They built cathedrals and made holy icons to let the faith live with us through the ages. The articles of faith were defined there and the true faith was well proclaimed, laying clear memories for our guidance through long ages. In the last stanza, Jerusalem, the long lasting city and other interesting places and paths for us are fondly remembered. As kings and emperors had gone to witness and commemorate sites of blessedness, the poet invites us all to bless the name of this holy land, where our blessed Lord Jesus once did stand!

Flowers in the Forests is a short poem with five stanzas, but the narrative sounds autobiographical, with the summary: "One does not know what is good till he takes a start"!

Once a man in the clan of teachers, himself being a teacher, thought he was happy and at full ease, enjoying with his young pupils, reading from books, and climbing trees. But he realized that he was in wrong, and that he did not know he was destined to a new life, a new challenge and a new command. Was he now to take it up or not – this specific role to play in life's theatre?

Life never comes unchallenged; the road ahead is not always smooth and flat, but fields to plough and forests to mend. The teacher's son knew it only slowly. And one day he found entirely a new place, new people to live with, and new tasks and challenges to face! He was destined to watch new plants coming to growth - not dry forests, but flowers in blooming. He saw the path threatening at start. While going steadfast he felt sure and slowly found it pleasant and smart as it gave him joy that endures. In fact, 'one does not know what is good till he takes a start'!

Endless Labor is another short poem with five stanzas, envisaging the essence of life and its 'endless labor'. We see many nuggets of wisdom in this poem:

> Life is not all freedom but some discipline!
> God has not made just as I – but also we!
> Your freedom to hit will end where my nose begins!

All these rules of life really end where our safety begins.

One lives a long time and sees a little more. He gathers much experience to his store. Yet, the reality is that "he can lead the horse to the water, but he cannot really make it drink". Many prophets had died with a broken heart, and many gurus tried to impart their best wisdom. But life is not a bunch of rules stopping the flow; Life is "a matter of an ear to hear and heart to obey".

The poet thinks that when the Lord had made this world, He made a place for good and evil - like pouring them to flow each from a different pot. It is not easy to tell those two apart. He sums up his findings in the last stanza:

> After you have tried to make the world good

> And have labored to set the good from bad apart
> And saw only small progress in doing that
> Then you call it a day, leave it to God, and depart.

Your Merciful Visit is a short poem meditating upon the merciful visit of God, whom he calls 'my beloved Lord'. The first couple of stanzas depict the glorious visit of God in the sun and under the moon. Having taken His morning bath in the rays of the morning sun, the Lord comes in glorious light 'to bring greetings to me for the day'. Then, in the rounded fullness of the moon, He comes 'to let me bask' in His peaceful glow. Even in the swiftly running lightening path, which gives him a taste of His endless power, the poet testifies that the Lord appears and disappears, filling his heart with endless awe.

Finally, the amazing love of God, that counts us worthy of His visit, is exalted in the last stanza:

> O Lord, how to tell Your wondrous love!
> While resting Your wings in the widest realms,
> You still deem me worthy to make
> Your countenance briefly to shine upon me.

Our Enemy Fear is a short poem that exposes our enemy called 'fear'! It is the enemy of mankind from times immemorial. It kills our intention to the right act, makes us numb, and paralyzes our mind from firm decisions. Fear made Jonah to run away from his task; Fear drove away Jacob to flee from his home; Lot's wife fearing her loss looked back; and with fear of death Peter tried to leave Rome.

Fear warns us from coming pain. But often it is fear of the unknown that drives us repeatedly to despair, like the ship going down even before the storm. Christ said to His disciples – 'Fear not':

> Set your hearts steady and your minds in peace
> When storms rise and thunders roaring heard
> It is I who is coming to you walking on the waves.

Do Not Despair is a short poem with six stanzas propounding the faith to see God's wonders, nullifying despair. The poet exhorts not to despair or to fret, for, the Lord is with us always:

If you fall in deepest pit
He will lift you now from it

If you have strayed like a fool into the deep forest, He will come in search for you and bring you to safety. When stormy winds blow on you, He will stand beside you. So rain or wind or roaring storm will not dare to harm you. He who had risen from death clothes you firmly with immortality and everlasting life.

Once His people had to cross the Red Sea and its huge high mass. The almighty raised his hand and showed the dry land through the sea. If you have the faith to see God's wonders where you are:

Cloudless eye and wholesome ear
These we need to see and hear.

He Called Me is a five-stanza poem presenting a call to salvation. Once the poet was in the wilderness searching for peace but God showed kindness upon him and called him. He thought he knew the way to life but he knew not he was blind. In the thickness of his hard strife he thought that he found the way.

Just like a long lost son in his sins, his soul has died. At last he found that he was wrong and bitterly cried aloud. God then like a good shepherd came and found him roaming in the wild. He risked His life to bring him home as His child. Who can forget such a great salvation tale? Night and day on the mount and vale he would tell for his joy and for the Lord as well.

The Wanderer is a short poem with satire. This is the story of two wanderers. The first one was wandering in a wilderness - lost and deserted! He could not find the way - not even a beaten track or a trodden footpath. As he did not know what to do and where to go, he found a man also like him looking out to find a way. He approached him seeking some help to get out of this hopeless wicked wilderness. The other wanderer then said to him that he was also like him, looking for a way out. Therefore he had suggested to him to try and find the way himself and that he shall do the same himself.

Teach Me Forgiveness is a short poem with five little stanzas. This is a plea to the Lord to teach. And it is appropriate to come to

Him for this as He alone is competent to teach us forgiveness. This five-fold plea is simple and sincere. The poet is asking the Lord to teach him to forgive as He has forgiven; to teach him to ignore insult whoever has done. He further asks the Lord to help him to forget injustice if done to him, just like it was done to Him on Calvary.

Because we are all sinners - both his opponent and he - if we ask tooth for tooth, there is not His love in us. It is time to see Jesus who has humbled Himself and became a poor servant sent by God to bear our sins and to grant Salvation. It is not easy to forgive. It is called the 'hard virtue'. Therefore, let us all learn to forgive at His feet so that we walk in His footsteps till we meet Jesus in heaven!

Calm Down, Friend is a single stanza poem conveying a profound piece of counsel. The two-word *mantra* is to "Calm down". This friendly advice enables one to compose his calm and be strong and determined in the midst of insult or ignominy. It is not your only lot:

> You are not the first one in the world
> To be ill-treated by the others
> It had happened to Great Socrates
> And it has happened to Jesus Christ!

Conclusion

As Henry Van Dyke aptly pointed, poetry tends to be descriptive as well as reflective.[40] This volume is designed to deal with the poetry of Pulidindi Solomon Raj in his sunset years. As the present author finds many bits of wisdom in these lines, he has set himself to an analytical study of this anthology, and the outcome is personally rewarding to him. The poetry of Solomon Raj, in these poems, as in all of his other works, is descriptive and reflective. It is hoped that this would bless the reader, through its didactic contribution and impact.

It was when Solomon and his dear wife were celebrating their diamond jubilee of their wedding that the author got to meet them after a long time, and could spend some quality time with the family. Solomon took all the visitors on a tour of his Ashram and was introducing his art works. It was the first ever exposure of Solomon's art to the present author, and he was captured by the artistic genius of Solomon Raj. Especially fascinating were the series of Solomon on 'Liberation in Luke's Gospel'! That was the starting point of the author's interest in Solomon's art, which led to an exciting journey of nearly two decades and continuing!

God Bless Moses Kumar! is a tribute from Solomon Raj on the occasion of the Diamond Birthday of Moses Kumar, who is the son of Solomon's elder sister. Solomon is glad that this nephew had won his heart soon that he wonders:

> Maybe we both sing the same song
> As we both walk with God along!

Solomon is happy that Moses Kumar has taken his father's path to serve the Lord in greater faith and that God has accepted his offer

40 Henry Van Dyke et al.: *Poetry: Descriptive and Reflective Verse.*

and made his work prosper. He describes how the Lord gave Moses Kumar a life partner who has guided him in prayer, and the offspring like heavenly stars, who made them twice blessed grand parents.

When Solomon wanted a bright scholar to bring his ministry to light God has moved Moses Kumar's heart to join him and share his part. Solomon appreciates his scholarship, and his deep perception:

I know the Lord blessed your pen
All the *pundits* saw your writings.

As Moses Kumar passes his sixtieth milestone, Solomon assures that God will never leave him alone, but make his harvest yet tenfold till he holds his crown in his hands. Solomon presents his song to Moses, with blessings ninety and nine in the name of the Lord:

Sixty times sixty be your share
In God's blessing both here and there
Angels do play their harpy strings
Praising God and bring you laurels!

The author, beyond being grateful for the wonderful heritage, wonders still as to how the grace of God richly dwelt in the life of Solomon Raj and how he was enabled to scale many pinnacles of accomplishments through his 'pen and the paintbrush'! "A thing of beauty is a joy forever" – said John Keats. The author never ceases to be amazed by the depths of meaning and heights of beauty in Solomon's works !!!

Appendices

A) List of Compilations of Solomon's Poetry

Part 1: Early Poetry of An Octogenarian

A) On Mundane Themes

1. Deep Sleep
2. Heavenward Way
3. A Friend
4. Paper to Write
5. Digging for Water
6. Out From the Waters

B) On Religious Themes

7. I Heard A Voice
8. Faith and Works
9. Holier Than Thou
10. The Sinful Woman
11. The Blessed Pebbles
12. The Passing Experience
13. Resurrection

C) On Philosophical Themes

14. A Bird in the Cage
15. The Sparrow and the Peacock
16. Honey Bees
17. Luxury of A Lovely Rose Garden

111. The Story of the Ladder
112. Ears to Hear
113. What Do We Seek?
114. Seeing and Hearing
115. Daily Prayer
116. Song of A Little Lamp
117. Pilgrims
118. Flowers in the Forests
119. Endless Labor
120. Your Merciful Visit
121. Our Enemy Fear
122. Do Not Despair
123. He Called Me
124. The Wanderer
125. Teach Me Forgiveness
126. Calm Down, Friend
127. God Bless Moses Kumar!

B) Early Poetry of An Octogenarian

1. Deep Sleep

Rest a while with eyes closed
Aside, all your burdens lay
A mantle of deep sleep on you hovers
Stay a while that way
Wait for a fresh dawn rising
The past has gone, it does not stay
For you have now a new path to walk.

2. Heavenward Way

Rest a while, close your eyes
All your burdens lay aside
Dream holy dreams if at all you can
Sleep, sleep peacefully
Till you awake and see
The glorious sun once again
Wipe away your saddening pain

3. A Friend

I had a long time dear friend
With whom often I had
Happy time spent.
Shared joys singing together
Then after some time
My friend severed his friendly ties
I did not ask why
I soon forgot the story
And said the bamboo flute
Does not sing the same sweet song
always.

4. Paper to Write

Bless the hands that invented paper
Think of a day without paper costly or cheaper
Paper and pen the working tools of a literate man
Day and night to enable him his thoughts to scan.

Paper is smooth lovely to caress and to kiss
As artist and writer I do not want to miss
Paper to write, paper to read, roll away or wrap
Or festival paper that many children wear as cap.

Paper on the kitchen table to wrap and mop
Paper to write and paint on my tabletop
Paper to beautify the living room wall
Paper not to miss on the toilet stool.

But the story of paper is ever so great
Starting with parchment from the skin of a goat
Passing through the weeds of the sunlit sea
And other things like the skin of mulberry.

Bamboo is great for paper of many kinds
And the pulp of rice hay in all kinds of grinds
Chinese made paper first long ago I am told
God bless them and India then followed.

5. Digging for Water

Once I saw a poor old man in the wood
Digging for water to quench his thirst
He grabbed the tools as good as he could
And started with a crowbar first

He went on and on like in a big race
With his brows wet and full with sweat
Hoping to strike water soon in that place
In his palms also some blisters he got

We do not know the reason why
He struck no water for which he did try

6. Out From the Waters

Rice fields, irrigation channels
A small wooden bridge
Across the fast flowing canal
Do I cross?
Can I cross the small channel?
I went slowly along
Holding fast
My grandmother's hand
She ahead and I behind
Oh, what happened?
I was down in the channel
Once my head under the water
And once quickly up for moment
As I struggled long at last
With my hands to the bank of the
Shallow channel
I knew with great relief
That I was still alive

7. I Heard A Voice

I heard a voice
A voice still and small
Coming out from
Somewhere deep
I do not know
Whether I was asleep
Or awake
I wish I had a piece of paper
To write the message
Down and read

8. Faith and Woks

A simple matter to begin with
To think of what I know about faith
It sounds so simple to the ear
It is so difficult if we want to know its depth.
Is faith the fruit or is it the root?
Does faith precede or follow good works?

It was clear to Dear Martin Luther
Who tried hard to us to make it clear
Because often men make some good deeds
And think that it is faith, all that it needs

If one can do good works all perfect
Like some unwisely think in effect
Why a God and faith in such a God
If we can do all that is needed without God

9. Holier Than Thou

Once I saw a big fat man
Going around in his soiled clothes
With his raiment dirtier than
The dust on the road on which he walks

Then along there came the same way
Another one in still murkier dress
As his arms are contaminated sway
A little man who was also in a mess

Hello friend, the big man called
Stopping the stranger on a side of the walk
Your clothes are dirty and all soiled
Go and wash them and then come back

All this is like the well known old story
When the frying pan called the tea-pot black

So the poor little man did not any more tarry
And fled from there and never came back

In fact the big man did not know
That he was as bad as the other fellow
Like a man with a big log in his eyes
Sought to help another with a speck in his.

10. The Sinful Woman

We do not know her name
She came in uninvited
To the Pharisee's home
While the guests sat at their dinner
She heard about the One who could
Wipe away her sins and give her a new life.
Had she heard him
Speak to the crowds elsewhere?
She went straight to the table
She touched His feet
Wept and washed them
With her tears,
Wiped them with her tresses
And anointed them
With great perfume
Breaking the jar.
But
One person was offended
Because she
Was a sinner.
Another man was deep in anger
Because the
Costly perfume
Was wasted, others, simply stared.
But the Lord –
He knew what she did and why

He declared that
What she had done
Shall be remembered
Wherever
The Good news shall be.

11. The Blessed Pebbles

The blessed pebbles
Of a forlorn and forgotten Land
Burning in the red hot sun all day
Immersed with deep sorrow
Wept sadly and wiped their tears
The soldiers walked holding spears
The women covered their faces in agony
Wind blew wild and the trees shook with fear
As the prophet of Nazareth
Came to that place called skull
Carrying dreadful cross on his shoulders
Walking with reddened feet
To be killed slowly on the cross.

12. The Passing Experience

The cross, the spear, the centurion
Sights we have in our memory's path
From what had happened
Long ago.
They can also be real in real life
For some of us.
They are often kept hidden
In the deeper Depths
Of the devotee's heart.

13. Resurrection

When I go to my final sleep
I shall surely awake and rise again
And jump out of the pit
To go the way which Jesus had gone

I shall not be among the dead
Never to me a second death
He sealed His promise with His blood
And that will be my second birth.

14. A Bird in the Cage

There was once a bird in the cage
It always wanted to hear a message
Of praise, praise and always praise.
It wanted all people around only this song to raise
About its wisdom, beauty and goodness
This bird wanted to hear this more and not less
From all its friends who gathered around
This same song the bird wanted to sound

Such a favor for some time the bird did find
But truly people are not always blind
There came one day some persons who could tell
That life is a mixture of good and bad as well
This, of course one day we all too should see
Because in fact that is what life should be.

When the bird heard this message
It got a shock and fell dead in the cage.

15. The Sparrow and the Peacock

The sparrow was very sad one day
How I wish that I like the peacock way
With plumes so colorful and ever so bright
Catching up the sun's daily light

But then one day the hunter came along
With his net to get the birds for a simple song
He cast the net on both the birds for a prize
But the sparrow escaped thanks to its small size

A bigger mane is not always at gain
Or a colorful plumage is good for the mien
So thank God for the way you're made to live
And never seek for more fancies and grieve.

16. Honey Bees

The busy tiny honey bees
Buzzing all around the trees
Dipping into the flowery womb
To get honey for the honeycomb.

Hopping in and hopping out
Do they know the truth about
What they're doing by and by
To make the trees multiply?

17. Luxury of A Lovely Rose Garden

Once I was in a rose garden lovely and gay
With the joy of sweet flowers and their flavors
How I wished there forever to stay
Enjoying some life's great pleasures.

But then I did not know to my dismay
That life is not all unmitigated pleasure
For man to enjoy as much as he may
But life is both sun and rain in some measure.

18. Transitory

Walking along the fields one day
I saw a lovely water pool
Not far away along the way
Making the place pleasantly cool

Wherein I saw a lotus - in full bloom
And green leaves spreading all around
It scattered to winds all my lonely gloom
What a great joy in it I found.

A few days later I went the way again
Hoping to see anew the beauty for a moment
Alas for me in the previous night's rain
The lotus lost all its glorious raiment

So all lovely things should one day go
Leaving perhaps only an inward chime
For, Nature had been designed so
For us to enjoy new things from time to time.

19. Lotus Flower

Lotus is the queen of flowers to us all the time
Bringing to mind symbols deep and sublime
Emerging out from the deepest darkness
It rises up towards the sunshine's brightness
Sprouting in time from it's dormant root
Almost from death into life does it upwards shoot.
I salute you thrice O lovely bloom
You remind me of new life from deadly gloom
To leave the darkness and rise towards the light
Is to reach the wisdom's heavenly height.

Once I made a picture showing lovely you
Floating in the distant waters of the river Nile blue
I do not know whether you're really there
Or it's my dream that you should be everywhere.

20. The Sorrowing Banana Stalk

Once there was a tall banana stalk
It started one day to itself talk
What a life, what a life, it said
Standing all day in the watery mud

To become mother bear fruit just once
And then to be cut up cast out by the fence
After that I am fully and surely forgotten
Giving my place to someone else then.

Look at the mango tree, it stands
Year by year its wide wing expands
Every summer decked in golden flowers
Perennially its sweet fruit it gives.

In its spreading branches now
Bees to visit and birds to live

Humans too desire its cool shade
As the hot days rage winds invade.

As the banana stalk spoke in its heart thus
The one above has heard these words thus
And he decided to turn all the bananas
At once to turn into big mango trees.

But people did not want only mangoes
Which come just in summer days
But they crave also for the banana fruit
Which they can all the year round get.

21. Love the Trees!

I love the trees because they are my friends
They keep company with us in all kinds of winds
It is hard to imagine a tree-less earth
Trees are with us from our very birth.

I like to sit under my mango tree
With its sweet smelling blooms calling the honey bee
I can never forget the taste of the king of fruits
At the end of summer mango almost every one eats.

Many sweet kinds of it in our great land
Name after name like *rasalu* and *dilpasand*
We await the season for the mangoes to come
And we want to taste all of them or at least some.

22. The Alone

On the deep sea beach
Seeing the sail boats
Lazily waving and

Not going anywhere
Shells at my feet waiting
To be picked

Or in the silent woods
Not far away
Where the sound of
The ominous bird
Is heard some times

Or on the hay stack
Which the harvesters
Have left behind
Nice and warm
In the early morning
Winter sun

I forgot to eat my fried nuts
In the brown paper bag
In all this there is no lonely place
However much I wanted
For me.

23. A Square Peg in A Round Hole

To put kind words in an uncouth mouth
Joyful thoughts in a hapless heart
And with kind words to mend a rebellious fool
Is really hard to do
Like trying to drive
A square peg in a round hole.

24. The Kite

The lovely kite that I now hold
In pretty colors green and gold
Up above the end of the line
Swaying in a nice inline
Wagging tail to the wind to sway

O, my kite, you perhaps know
While you are high up and I am low
The string that holds together us both
Helps us to be together in truth.

25. The Signboard

Do you see me
I just mean see not read
See long enough to know
What I say
I am a new incarnation
A better one than
The little string which people used
To remember their arithmetic
I am not ashamed
If ignored
I'm told the Egyptians
Before they used small pictures
To send and receive messages
Before they had hieroglyphics.

26. Door Called Dwar!

Door or dwara is a means strong and stout
To keep us always in and others out
At the same time we are also clearly told
That we invite friends with open doors manifold.

There are garden doors to keep goats straying
Doors to the bed room to keep any Toms peeping
And doors of steel, barbed wire and iron grill
To keep thieves out from their mischievous drill.

We are also told to keep the doors open
To our minds so knowledge advent may happen
Our hearts open to let our love keep flowing
And our affection gets always growing.

Open minds help avoid prejudices great and small
But open mouths may cause conflicts to one and all
So the wise men for us have always strained to instruct
That we know when to open the door and when to shut.

27. Awake or Asleep

Were you awake or asleep
Talking with that man
Do you know
Whether he is real or a phantom?
Pinch yourself and see
Some people see
What they want to see
Sometimes a strange experience
Stays as part of yourself
For a little longer
But some times
It moves off like a cloud
Does in the path of the
Wind.

28. Light Sleep

I sleep very lightly
Most of the time
Partly awake and partly asleep
And what do I see in such a stage?
Is it all real as in real life
And what happens to such so called
Experience?
Is it something which had
Happened already,
Or is it something foreboding?
If neither –
Then what is it?
If it is one of these
What is its meaning?

29. Darkness

I asked a wise man once
To help me from my loneliness
And then he told me that I need
Some good company indeed
Can I know, for instance
How good the company is in advance?
No, you have to test and see
How good the company be
Then if it's not to my taste
Can I leave the group in haste?
No, it is not easy at all
Once you in a bad company fall.

30. Breath Control

Once I taught Indian religions in USA,
To a batch teen age boys and girls.
And the topic one day was yoga practice
Introducing my lesson I said -
'To practice yoga we have to learn
Breath control'
Then there was a great confusion
On the faces of my young pupils
I stopped there and made some
Careful enquiries
Then I knew that they thought
I was talking about 'Birth Control'
Instead of 'Breath Control'.

31. Life is Like A Train Journey

Life is like a quickly running train journey
People come and people go
Some of them look happy
But some do not appear so

Once in a while you see a smile
Just to make you feel at home
But if it doesn't come for awhile
You may still get in the next mile.

32. A Trimmed Quill

Never say for a moment
That you were not born
With a trimmed quill in your hand
The tree had no fruits when
It is planted

A sword cannot cut
Till it is heated red in the fire
And beaten with a hammer
A work of brain
Is half brain and the rest is strain
So said Solomon Raj.

33. Seeking Support

Weak souls seek support
Like a tiny creeper needs
To reach its proper heights
But a solid tree stands
On its own
Like a seasoned oak tree trunk
Facing all the rain and strain

Giving and taking some help
Is not unwise
Like a mighty gun will need a cartridge
To hit the target right
So once said Solomon Raj.

34. Thankfulness

In the morning I threw some grains
Under the porch
For birds to come and peck their fill
Crows and song birds and others came
And I was really happy to see them
Some birds so gaily pecked at the grain
All others have followed doing the same
And then they all took to wings and flew away
But the song bird stayed on and sat in the garden tree
And started singing sweet songs for me.

35. Love is Long-Suffering

Love is said to be long suffering
It does not jump to its feet too soon
When things go wrong some times
Love takes time to think and do
Like the sun rises only after
The night is gone.

36. Love Reality

Love is by definition mutual
One gives it and the other receives
And the one who receives love
Does also gives it back
Happily to the one who first gives
But loving one's self is quite different
It is that a person gives to himself
Trees bear fruit but do the trees ever
Consume their own fruit in hunger?

37. I and Others

I am the first and all others next
So thought once an unwise man.
Only my opinion in the world is the best
No one can think as best as I can
But then came one better than him.

38. Company and No Company !

Cherish the company of all your friends
Who come and join as the journey extends
But stop fretting when they depart
Just like they came to join you at the start.

It happens again along the way
Some people join and some go away
Till your journey comes to an end
Till you yourself say goodbye to every friend.

Life's journey runs this way
Meeting friends along the way
One comes to you and the other goes
This is what life's experience shows.

Do not think that any one is unkind
Leave a sweet thought about every friend
Because all friendships are transitory
It is good to accept and cherish a sweet memory.

39. Agree or Disagree

Once I thought that all should feel
Just as I do and not differ a great deal.
But soon I found that it's not so easy
To expect every one see just as I see.

We are not the same stuff all of us
Since creation was not planned that way.
Different ways are the sole beauty of life
Also between the husband and wife.

If the potter made all pots the same,
In size and shape color and name
His would be a dull creation indeed
To which really no one would heed.

So I have learnt slowly with a smile
That others disagree with me once in a while
Therefore it is wise for all people to see
What the other person's opinions would be.

40. Show Each Other the Way !

Once I saw a lovely little girl pretty and fair
She loved me too and came with me her life to share
She agreed with me in life with all things most often
But she had to differ with me now and then
This had never been a block to our mutual love
Because we never thought of the one over the other above
Two of God's creation each in our own way
One always to show the other the life's way
It is good for me to have some one to say - no
When I sometimes, as often, go astray.

C) Early Poetry of A Nonagenarian

41. Sonnet

Village life and milk from cows at the dawn
Small water brook in front of little house
Among others clustered in the green lawn
This is where Raj started his life so nice

Some friends to play when it isn't school time
Or graze the cattle in midday hot sun
Singing folk songs of joy and dance to rhyme
Chasing each other and then on to run

Raj comes always somewhat late for his lunch
Unless he is away on a long trip
Or all his friends ran away to the beach
To see on the sea a sailing new ship.

This is the way their life happily spending
Raj and his friends escaped proper tending.

42. A Village Boy

Once I was a village boy so happy
Jumping playing swimming at the sea shore
Climbing trees and picking fruits in plenty
I never did care for a thing no more.

The earth, the sun, the wind and water cool
The calf and cow the grassy fields I love
With them I played and friendly would I feel
These are the gifts we all get from above.

The one who is blind to these gifts of God
Is surely poor and much joy he does miss
His life is surely dull and real sad
So we always these gifts of God relish.

Sweet creation He has given to us
So we thank Him He made us prosperous.

43. Adwaitha

What is it to "be united with" God?
Is it possible that it will happen
While still we are here and remain human
Or does it happen after death indeed?

The soul for release from body does plead
Seeking some kind of freedom to happen
And the feeling of distance be undone
What is oneness with God for us indeed?

True *aikya* should happen on earth truly
In prayer and constant meditation
This leads to the oneness with the Holy
God is God and man is nothing but man.

God is to be enjoyed like sweet sugar
But what joy if man himself becomes sugar.

(So I like 'I and thou' relationship with God
Rather than being lost in him)

44. The Alcoholic

Foolish man drowning deep in alcohol
You lose your senses and forget your shame
Do you know that what you earn is bad name?
Open your eyes before turning a fool.

Can't you pause in your life a while and think?
Life should never become a wasted game
Better kill your passions, bring them to tame
Before you soon in a deadly pit sink.

Causing pain to parents and the partner
It haunts you all your life like a big ghost
And on deathbed you find no peace ever
In endless flames you will surely be lost.

In the name of a wicked and poor drunkard
Going unwept unsung and unremembered.

45. Early Rising

Early to bed and early too to rise
Was something which the primitives have done
Simpler than this as a rule they have none
Whether this made them healthy, wealthy, wise

Or not this rule was considered wise.
We're sure this saying was not meant for fun
By this during day more work could be done
And so this to us is not a mighty surprise.

Lifestyles have drastically changed so
Nighttime is so pleasant to some people
To rise with the sun to them is trouble
I guess life has to be happily lived also.

Early to rise is not a big gospel
To stick to this old rule is impossible.

46. Two Kinds of Friendship

God-fearing friends are always good to have
For counseling and for time for prayer too
But never for the worldly chatting nave
Which create rivalries and sadness too.

To pray with fellow believers is bliss
With God to spend some time with them is good
So that they and you to each other wish
His love and abundant peace and sainthood.

When you with friends sit in prayer worship
Let not worldly chat ever enter in
Only seek Almighty God to worship
And live with Him and have His name within.

Believers do bring glory to His name
Worldly assemblies are another game.

47. Giving and Receiving

We help others in need and this we know
'Tis more blessed to give than to receive
This is true because the Bible tells so
We give ourselves to God and too alms give

The Son of God gave Himself for our sake
Humbled Himself to become a Servant
In our place the cross to willingly take
Is this not the Gospel which God had sent?

This great salvation which we have received
We share with all nations and bear witness
O this message all over be proclaimed
And the Lord's kingdom on earth shall progress

So the Lord God is the greatest giver
And His name be praised now and ever.

48. Joy With Children

I always thought it a wonderful thing
To have children and with them to enjoy
With children to play and their skills employ
More blessed than this there can be nothing.

To feel proud of them as they are growing
But it is not easy to our minds apply
All expected comforts for them to supply
Or help them to succeed in life achieving.

God should enable them to a worthy life
To set a model for others to live
And prove their chivalry in the world's strife
And to the parents a helping hand give.

This we should pray for and always desire
But this we can from God only aspire.

49. Tent on the Highest Rock

I shall with the help of the Lord
Pitch my tent on the highest rock
That to me was His faithful word
That in this I should His hand seek.

Only the best and noblest mount
For my bliss and the greatest joy
In this I shall never count
The cost I in this walk employ.

God for us sure designs the best
As He gives me a heart to seek
Although I pass the path hardest
Who can tell me that I am weak.

Do I need an assurance still
To make it true that He's with me.

50. The Sinner and His Song

Old Adam's seed is in my blood
I keep erring always
Till one day I shall reach sainthood
I have to watch my pace.

But O, my soul, just wait in peace
Sinners have God's promises
In His blood He washed and keeps
Till I reach paradise.

Hence on earth I live in solace
Which the Lord to me gives
I shall get cure for my disease
And my soul with Him lives.

Angels and saints raising the song
Praising the Lord our God
I shall join them and walk along
With my Lord ever glad.

51. The Stroke Dealt by God

How blessed it is to be struck by God
Struck deaf dumb and also darkening blind
This stroke is what our souls will truly need
So that but only through faith Him we find.

Sight and speech, and touch the gift of hearing
God gave us as tools of sense perception
When God strikes a blow they disappear
And only then faith will begin action.

Sensory thoughts some bitter some pleasant
We keep getting constantly through these doors
They go only so far and then prevent
Us to view the glories of heavenly shores.

Christ was blind to earth-bound empty glory
Was blind to pleasures and bodily pain
He was mute when He had the cross to carry
The burden of our sin and awful stain.

We the humans are slaves of our senses
Seeking blindly but we know well that we
Till the Lord will strike us dead in senses
Are blind to what God wants us all to see

And deaf to what God wants us all to hear.

52. Who is He?

Who is He and what is He
Could He John the Baptist be
Is He Elijah the great
Who rode in fire chariot?

Who is He as people say
Look up to Him in what way
Rabbi, Scribe or Pharisee
How the people do Him see?

He was not the forerunner
But He was the true Savior
Not the chariot rider He
But came to save you and me.

Once a woman at the well
Could not easily Him tell
Nicodemus had perceived
Signs and miracles He showed.

Greater than all these was He
Simon Peter once could see
By the prompting of the Lord
Him the only Son of God.

53. Redemption from Pain

Pain is common to all humans
Sadness is the rule of life
Crying is how life does commence
And all life's journey is a strife.

From some pain and even disease
Even kings are not immune
Forbearance and silence helps us
To endure some of the pain.

Saints and sages have gone through this
Often tear some and sad path
They have set some hope for some bliss
And all pain is not God's wrath.

There will be an end to suffering
Some day if not soon may be
Man is not made just for weeping
But one day relief to see.

54. Waiting for A Harvest

I labored on a barren field
Seeking a generous yield
Sowing, growing and waiting
As farmers sure be doing.

Some thought it was mere waste
Others thought it a bad taste
And that I was too crazy
For not taking life easy.

In despair I left the field
Which they thought will never yield
But the Lord then woke me up
And said I should not give up.

I came back and worked along
Within my heart a sweet song
Worked again in the same place
With the sun right in my face.

Working thus I prayed to God
To whom there is nothing hard
He sent clouds and rain along
That made the crop green and strong.

My harvest then plentiful
All my barns came breaking full
I knew God will give the fruit
If I worked and afraid not.

55. Love and Respect

Love and respect should come from man's inside
Naturally sprung flowing like river
A gift from God and a bond to abide
Blessing both receiver and the giver.

The Canaanite Ruth had freely shown it
To Naomi in love her life submit
God in His love has firmly sealed it
A seal that lead to the Savior's advent.

Genuine love is God's own blessed gift
Like the blossom and its sweetest odor
Never in the sands of time going drift
Day by day to grow and duly prosper.

Love is such that is born of God's design
So like the Divine Lily brightly shine.

56. Brothers Living Together

How good for brothers to live together
Under one and the same roof as it were
If the wives do not fight with each other
And share life's blessings always together.

How Christ-like to live in brotherly love
Coming from different realms whatever
Share with each other God's gifts from above
This is what a brother does to brother.

Trinity the symbol of God's oneness
In three persons but really one God
Thus our God has revealed His presence
A call to us for godly brotherhood.

So His people live as His one body
Till they be with Him in heaven one day.

57. When My Heart Went Astray

When my heart went astray running wildly
Like an elephant which has gone astray
In the forest trespassing all the way
The Lord my God subdued it so kindly.

He with His goad had soon controlled my heart
Subduing my unwilling rude spirit
And He to take hold and ever rule it
And from me He kindly never depart.

O, what a rest I have now to enjoy
And He on Him my cares always employ
No more stress and waywardness too abroad
And no more snares and temptations too hard.

In His home I find the needed safety
And stay with Him through all eternity.

D) Later Poetry of A Nonagenarian

58. The River

Trickle by trickle through
The narrow crevices of the
Mountainside
Now hiding behind the stones
And now showing up again
Creeping down in curvy lanes
While other such small streams
Join it along the way.
Down it swiftly comes
Along the mountainside
And as it reaches a sharp edge
Off it jumps making a thundering sound
Into the gorge below
Uprooting shrubs to drag them along its way
And turning around the rebellious trunks
Rooted firmly standing along its way
Polishing the smaller pebbles
Breaking down some bigger stones
Raising clouds of foams at last it meets
The motherly belly of the deep mountain valley

59. Crossing the River

The river in its native wild fury
Creeping crawling jumping along its way
Along the mountain slopes crossing hurdles
Turning around big bumps of boulder
Leaping into the valley raising a cloud of mist
And a rainbow in the sky above.

Flows in to slower gentle plainly land
Grows slower and wider to left and right
Looking like a mighty native lake.
Now it calmly tends to further slow down

Slowed by the big earthen dams across
Now it is easier to cross by sailboat.

Take a trip on one of the big sailboats
Laden to the brim with dry coconuts
Kept in course with a mighty big rudder
Going forward with the help of the wind
When it nearly reaches the edge
The boatmen held it and pulled to barge
How happy we were to have crossed the river.

60. Childhood Memories

Living in past memories is wonder
Recalling events is too a game
For some of them we go faster
For some of them it is never the same
Like once when I was walking
Through the rice fields, Andhra's fame
I went ahead grandma's hand holding
I was so sure like was playing a game.

Before I knew what happened
From the narrow foot-bridge I walked
Into the flowing channel I slipped
Poor grandma into knee-deep water she waded
To her great joy from water me she saved.

61. The Amazing Spring

The sweetest birds do sing
The hills response giving
The spotted deer running
In the sweet pleasant spring.

My heart is rejoicing
With the green branch swinging
Mine joy is quite rising
While experiencing.

My soul along will sing
With jasmine branches swing
My lower chin dropping
For beauty of the spring.

62. Hatching Bird's Eggs

The cool early dawn
In the ripe corn field
Sitting on the wooden munch
Under the shade of coconut palms
My job was then to scare
The stray birds because the crop was ripe.
The open straw-bed was rather warm
My younger sister brought for me
A pot of cool rice water
She was sleeping still
On the munch, the poor girl
The faithful dog has gone to chase
The intruding fox.

I decided to climb the tree nearby
And hunt for birds' nests
And slowly brought one down with a few eggs
To cover them up and watch hoping they hatch
In another twenty days
Bird on the tree and man on the earth
Are always better of course.

63. Floating in the Air

In dream sometimes I fly in the air
And then I like to stay right there
But soon I drop to earth like a stone
And find myself on earth alone.

Flying feeling gives a wisp of joy
Then sadness comes like a broken toy
Bringing me back to where I was
No joy, no wonder, and no bliss.

64. The Toothless Smile

I watched for a little while
The toothless baby's sweetest smile
And the sparkling stars in her eyes
I thought that she was cute and wise.

Her fists so tightly closed as if
Starting to face the life-long strife
Her feet straight up like dancing
Even now taking a swing.

I felt so happy within myself
For such a sweetest little new life
And breathed within me a blessing
To God for making her life to me a song.

65. A Lazy Summer Afternoon

A lazy summer afternoon
Time does not pass so soon
Wet all over the body
With a humid kind of sweat
Hard to sit, hard to stand

Not so easy to understand
No use with two ceiling fans
They would simply go to dance
Good to send some fair
Only some warm air
Getting unrobed? But to what limit
In the sweltering gloom
Of the hot summer afternoon.

66. Sugarcane Plantation

Sweetly it smells lovely it looks
The fertile large sugarcane field
Rows upon rows the canes grow tall
Till to the cutter's sickle they yield.

The farmers cut the cane and hacks
Dressing and cleaning the dry leaves
Laying them straight in neat big packs
Then send into crushing mill wheels.

At a safe distance the oven glows
In big hot metal pan boiling
Sweet sugar cane juice thickly simmers
Then poured into cans for cooling

Thus goes how sugar cane harvest
Cut denuded sent to be crushed
Boiled in big vats poured in blocks
Black sugar comes by this process.

We, village boys enjoy all this
Wisely we there loaf around, see
Kindly the worker cuts a piece
And throws at us happily to chew.

67. Kondpally Wooden Man

Kondpalli-made wooden man
Forget you who ever can
Hands and feet too in all detail
Skillfully made up to scale.

Forest timber and carving tools
These with skill have made us fools
Made with the carpenter's skill
So all our hearts with wonder to fill.

Your eyes like ours small and black
Staring at us as we once look back
As you daily standing where
We kept you with our art ware.

Transitory your life as ours
Made for some joy and then disappears
Contributing happiness
In this world of wilderness.

Birthday party when it comes
Why in the year comes only once
Often should come all good events
The day and date need not announce.

68. Song to the Koel

Welcome O, dear koel
Perched on the green mango tree
Nothing in the world stops your singing
To us your joyful spring song.

Even dreadful winter rain
Or the blowing eastern wind
Can stop you proclaiming
To us that summer is around.

Welcome to you dear koel
Coming from the freezing north
Stay with us as long as you want
The melody of your song is sweet.

We praise you little koel
You conqueror of misery
The music of your sweet song
Redeems us from sadness.

When you leave us here dear koel
You come to see us once again
To feed us with your sweet song
And to relieve us from our woes.

69. Black Coffee

When I sleep well tucked in bed
In the night after I was well fed
I sometimes dream of the black coffee
Which of course, in the morning I hate to see.

This some people like to drink
It keeps them awake from sleep they think
They relish its bitter taste
But I think that it is all a waste.

70. Houses to Live

A house to live is gift of God
Some of us receive
We do not know the reason why
Some have no place to live.

Some command spacious palaces
But some not e'en a hut

Poverty the child of injustice
But poor man's fault 'tis not.

Unjust distribution of wealth
Does make some people poor
Complaints, sit outs, and agitations
Cannot provide the cure.

71. Wealth to Show Mercy

The poor leper at last died
And also died the rich man
One went to the blissful side
But not so the other one.

We may ask why it was so
One was patient in his faith
The other did only know
To drown deep in worldly wealth.

Wealth for us to show mercy
We poor humans do forget
At the end we try to see
But the door then shall be shut.

72. The Bazar

City roads and dusty wind
Crowds moving all around
Shopping loafing, sightseeing
Even some lazy walking
How much more
To walk around
In the city dusty bazar
Walking on the melting coal tar.

73. Meetings and Conferences

Meetings, consultations,
Conferences and agendas
Chairmen, presidents
Welcomes and farewells.

Everything is to be done
Openly
Collectively
Democratically
And sometimes ecumenically.

Democratic discussions
Never one man's decision
But alas at the end
That happens as one man's way.

74. T. V. Preachers

Many anxious TV preachers now
Make me tired of the Gospel, which I love
They try to impress me with loud noise
What can be told in gentle voice.

Throat is their tool and volume their trick
Hoping the listener changed and quick
But seldom have they a tool to measure
How much the listeners got of the treasure.

The Gospel in fact is simple indeed
We try to make it heavy and try to feed
The lambs with meat while they only need milk
Meat instead of milk makes the poor lambs sick.

Preachers seldom have learnt the skill
Of teaching people with more good will
Using our Lord's beautiful fare
Of flowers o' the field and the birds o' the air.

75. Human Wild Beasts

Inhuman sometimes does man become
Committing tragic crimes
Hard to see and hard to overcome
The shock and shame it brings.

Some youth today have lost their soul
And forfeited their shame
Making all our poor conscience foul
And bringing to us bad name.

Rape and kill a poor virgin
In a fast moving bus
How sad and painful to imagine
And how greatly disastrous.

We feel the pain deep in our heart
And now we sure believe
That man is much worse than the beast
Which in the wilderness live.

A blooming life nipped in the bud
And a story told all the same
But never can our conscience stop
Grieving in agony and shame.

76. Troubles Come Together

Troubles come together and not alone
Like camels from father Abraham's house
If you to them kindness and love have shown
Like Rebecca great Isaac's gentle spouse

They take you home to the bridal palace
For which purpose the Father had sent them
For you to get abundant high solace
To be received with great royal acclaim.

This is great and good news sure to our life
To face problems when they come together
And to be prepared to face our own strife
And in His name to win Satan ever.

Defeat the foe with the sign of the cross
And inherit the great kingdom at last.

77. Camels are Coming

Camels come in a long big row
We do not chase them away
Give them water and mercy show
To God's home they know the way.

Camels are from the father's yard
He sends them to bring the bride
So that she comes happy homeward
And to his son be wedded.

Trials and pains are the camels
Treat them well with cool water
Put on them the proper saddle
They take you to the father.

In return to the food to the camels
Get gold bangles to your hands
And to the others in the house
There are gifts too and garlands.

Father and son bridegroom you know
Guide is the Holy Spirit
Trials like camels the way show
The right path to bride-groom's feet.

78. As the Wind Blows

As the wind blows gently
So the Spirit shows silently
Follow my soul, the Lord's leading

You will not falter in your step
Your goal you will not give up
If you in the Lord's path keep proceeding

He sends His angels
To keep you from dangers
And brings you to His home guiding

When perils do appear
And sadness comes too near
Lean upon His bosom believing

He is able and kind hearted
He knows too where you started
Your path He will all make straightened.

79. God's Ways Are Greater

Do not fret when things go wrong
And in your mouth there's no song
God knows what is good for you
His plans always great and true
Earthly kingdoms, which we know
When to them we great desire show
God's kingdom we do not see
Since our eyes are blinded be.

When Jesus died on the cross
His friends thought it was a loss
Desolate they went again
To fishing, their old bargain
Jesus then opened their eyes

Showed them that His rule will rise
Blessed are they who perceive
And His promises receive.

80. Blessedness of Loneliness

Human beings crave for company
Without which they feel vulnerable
Gift of speech providing communication
Is also for sure a great gift to mankind.

But both of these we may desire
Only in counted and small measure
Too much of these we don't aspire
Although they give a small pleasure

Evil company can lead to tears
Sharper tongue can burn like wild fire
Each of these two harmless appears
But soon the fun will disappear

One should sometimes sit silently
Trying to hear the still small voice
Which one can hear only quietly
Since we become deaf with noise

In waiting for God's presence
Our souls do get richly sustained
Only in the lonely spaces
The holy countenance can be seen.

81. Companionship

Human heart craves for company
Like nature will abhor vacuum
Loneliness is vulnerable
Speech is the greatest gift to men
To use it and communicate.
A silent person is either dumb
Or he is a sage in forest in silence
We are told that God in truth
Is always in communion
With the Son and the Holy Spirit.

82. Man is Not Made to be Alone

In blundering selfish pride
Like a wildest horse I ride
And called my friend a fool and then in remorse I wept.

He did not say a word
A response I never heard
It sharply pain seared through my heart like a bitter sword

In a coolest kindly mood
In the friendly way I ever had
I shared my love with a stranger lad and made him really glad

Humans are not made alone
In lonely burdens to only groan
The good Lord made them to each other's concerns made known

Our savior and the Lord Jesus
Came here to bear our woes
And gave his life as a ransom for all our sins on the cross.

83. Then and Now

I did not know your name
But often I saw you going this way
Once I tried to stop you and ask the same
So as to be your friend every day

Now that I know your name
And since I became your friend
Life now is no longer the same
We shall be friends till the end.

84. End of the Journey

Lord, as now my journey comes to an end
I come to Thy door bruised and wounded
With sores and cuts which You alone can mend
Now I come to Your gate greatly renowned.

When once, long ago You asked me to go
To work in Your vineyard with tools and wares
Never counting the costs I had done so
And You have taken on You all my cares.

When there was sadness I tried to sow joy
And where there was strife I tried to bring peace
Where there was greed there real contentedness
Which *mantra* St. Francis too did employ.

When I from people did not get acclaim
I went ahead and labored all the same.

85. Desirable Epitaph

Look, look my friend life is too short
You make the best of it now
In the task giv'n to you, work hard
Your stewardship skills now show.

What you leave on earth when you die
Not riches lands, not great wealth
But great life lived and virtue high
These will last and of great worth.

Do not fall in sloth and slumber
That will make your life a waste
Some have failed this to remember
Left nothing of any good taste.

Never stop to acquire wisdom
It helps to charter your path
And keeps you from sad falling down
Saves you too from nature's wild wrath.

Make friends in life do it wisely
Evil friendships are a pest
They can bring you great misery
Leading life to big unrest.

Not a lender nor a debtor be
So told once a wise man sure
Live within your means be thrifty
And share your cup with the poor.

When the call comes you go in peace
Your reward in God you'll see
And the life you have lived in grace
On your grave epitaph be.

86. Miracles

I do not seek a miracle to
Showing to men what God can do
He who wants a miracle crutch
Does not stand on his faith as such.

Unless we His commands fulfill
Miracles do stay far away still
Like a man builds his house on sand
Faith based on miracles does not stand.

Do not rejoice that you can do
Miracles, they will not benefit you
Rather see that your name is in
The Book of Life rightly written.

87. The Call and the Journey

When He said to me "come"
I didn't know what I get
But when I simply went to Him
What I saw was perfect.

He wanted me to leave
Some comforts of my own
But what great blessings He could give
To me till then unknown.

Great wine and living bread
More than I ever see
He kept in store to keep me fed
And make me rested be.

Fellowship of great lords
And company of saints
I did get as I went forwards
And royal rich garments.

My mouth was filled with song
Right along all the way
And I had strength right in my wing
To reach the clouds and stay.

88. Offerings

All my labors now have ended
My life with you Lord I've thankfully expended
And now comes the time of rest to me
I call upon You to come and help
So I forget all that belongs to self
And peacefully await Your face to see.

When now I reach my heavenly rest
I have no need for any worldly lust
All my needs in You are fully met
The whitest stone, Lord, that You will give
With a name known only to those that receive
Which alone in my strength I will never get.

All the promises I have lived to see
Are coming to be fulfilled now for me
Since the Lord has always been faithful
The glory in which He ever lives
And the everlasting peace He alone gives
I now begin to see in full.

I have seen along the way some flowers and also thorns
Several praises and a few scorns
Both I tried with Your help to bear
Your grace was enough for me to live
And peace which only You can give
While adding blessing on blessing to be sure.

That which I did and what I couldn't do
I remit humbly all my Lord, to you

And ask you to fulfill this for me
Your grace is wider than all my strife
Your love still greater all through my life
And now I come forever your face to see.

89. Old Age Comes

Good, old age has come at last
You do not run now so fast
Once or twice wake up at night
But late mornings will be right.

Take your time at the dining place
Chew and swallow, it is not a race
Talk along it's more pleasant
Do not sit and keep silent.

Wisdom is what you like to share
Even if others do not always care
Where should your experience go
If you to others do not show.

Do not try to crack hard nuts
Or your dentures break in bits
Soft and spicy let your food be
This is wise as you would see.

Do not welcome verbal duel
To bitterness it is sure fuel
Learn to say, Yes – always
Whatever the opponent says.

Look ahead to a peaceful end
People bid farewell and send
For a while if they remember you
Know it as an added blessing too.

90. To Be With My Lord

My desire is to be with my dear Lord
He is my good shepherd and a sure guide
I have his great promise and good firm word
Which long ago in his presence I heard

I shall steadfastly swim holding his hand
To cross the deep dark river and be safe
And surly reach my father's holy land
Where there is no more hard labor and grief

Singing songs in praise to God, I live there
Always angelic hosts with me to be
In perfect bliss and joy for ever share
This is what the Lord had promised to me.

91. Adoration

We offer our worship to God our Lord
Who created the heaven and the earth
And the depths of the space just by his word
To him we sing praises full of our mouth

His name is holy and worthy of praise
And adoration of heaven and earth
The whole creation for ever shall raise
Songs to him and adore him in faith

Reigning above and watching all creation
He receives praises of heavenly hosts
Responding to him in adoration
Declaring his might for ever that lasts

Worthy is the creator and our God
Worthy to be adored and be worshipped
Who keeps us safe by his staff and his rod
We declare his might with voices equipped.

92. How to Worship You My Lord?

How to worship you my Lord
And adore your lotus feet?
How to get your kindly word
Comforting and ever sweet?

What is pleasing to your heart
As a gift from me to thee?
With what offering I start
What is it you want from me?

Strange it is you never ask
Gold and silver or incense
You never try to make my task
Burdensome and more immense

Repentance and tearful heart
Reconciliation firm
These I offer to your feet
Forgiveness to me confirm

What offering you want most?
Willing heart and loving soul
These are pleasing to your taste
More than these you never call

Strange you never ask a gift
Since I am a pauper true
Fallen souls you surely lift
To give praise and honor you

Holy Francis your servant
Discarded his mantle robe
Shoe-less walked with gunny robe
Went to preach in sack raiment

A poor woman seeking grace
And forgiveness washed your feet

With her tears of deep disgrace
Poured perfume adoring treat

Bhakthi, Lord is what you seek
Ear to hear and mouth to praise
Seeking in thy path to walk
These as gifts to you we raise.

93. Beware Jonah

What a blessing it is for you to do
The task that the Lord has assigned to you
To take a ship going to Nineveh shore
To call people to repent, turn to God.

It is to Nineveh that He sent you
But if you ignore that job to pursue
And take a ship to safe Tarshis instead
Then God like a fisherman sends a whale.

With a whisper'd message to swallow you
Bring you back to tell Ninevites the tale
So men and all creatures return to God
Now you know how God cares for the people.

Like a farmer for dying garden weeps
You are hurt when the tree is dying now
Which you never planted nor have nurtured
How much more God cares when people perish.

94. Doubting Thomas

Doubting Thomas was not an agnostic
Saint and a great martyr as we know him
Asking questions and proofs heuristic
We poor humans we always do ask them.

Sunrise sunset and all, none suspects
Since we see them ever with us happen
Rising from death no one really expects
Only Jesus from death did rise again.

So did Thomas wanted to see by sight
This in a way is quite unwise in deed
For knowledge of God comes only through faith
Wisdom for that we will never need.

So Thomas the doubtful did never count
It a loss to ask visual proof to see Him
And he himself died for Christ on Thomas Mount
Among the apostles Thomas was one of them.

95. Woman At the Well

O woman, at the village solitary well
What thoughts in your heart and anxious soul?
With empty pot you came along the way
Seeking water from Jacob's blessed well.

Places to worship your creator and God
The great Gerizim your holiest mount
The kings and the great realms to make you glad
With them are you not content?

Meet Jesus who comes today here to you
And He can give to you what you seek
Freedom from hunger and liberty too
And all barriers too He will surely break.

Him you know as great Messiah you see
May He today your great savior be.

96. O Woman At the Well

O woman at the well
Standing alone and looking around
Do you know what you are looking for?
Perhaps about blessed commemoration
Of ancestors and their gifts
Or maybe you are searching to visit pilgrim centers.

One day you may have all these but
Still you are lost.
Better know what you need and ask for it
Better know what it is that you need most
And know who He is now speaking to you
And ask Him He will give.

97. Waiting Upon the Lord

When I prayed before my God
I talked all the time not He
Asking Him for all I need
But He has giv'n all to me

Therefore let me wait on Him
In silence to what He says.

I often prayed and asked the Lord
So I try and help myself
So far I am well and good
When I need I ask for help

If I waited on the Lord
He will do what I cannot.

I often tried to tell the Lord
Knowing not what He can give
Asked for petty things I need
But He can give so much more

So let me now wait on Him
For He gives more glorious gifts.

I in prayer told Him not
That I want to serve Him now
For His sake I do His will
If He kindly shows me how

I pray and wait on the Lord
Till He calls and lets me serve.

If now I wait on the Lord
I shall get my health renewed
Like an eagle flies upward
Running and never be tired

Walking fast I shall not fall
He shall leave me not at all.

98. Healing Comes from God

I sat with people in sickness
In deep and acute pain
Some wept and wailed in deep distress
And others simply moan.

To go over all misfortunes
And cry in too many words
Is the sign of a weak heart
It makes pain all the more worse.

Medicine helps to make pain less
And doctors have some cures
In spite of all our loud complaints
Only God our health restores.

99. Sickness and Health

Mortal body is made of clay
Breakable on any day
Brittle just like a mud-made pot
Shredded one day on the spot.

Lovingly kept with all great care
Nourished ever with good fare
No one knows why it gets so sick
And receives the painful prick.

When it gets into such a state
As much bitter as once so sweet
When it was quite healthy and hale
Riding joyful clouds and sail.

Sickness as we all know does strike
Both the rich and poor alike
Sometimes lasting long and so deep
Sometimes making shorter sweep.

Wind and rain even summer shine
Dirt and unclean food even
Often we do not know what brings
Torment to our healthy wings.

Man with sickness had fought too long
When medical skill was not so strong
Plagues and pestilences wiped the earth
Coffins carried or bodies burnt.

Men migrating fled from the plague
Solution to the problem looked vague
Men worshipped the trees and the brooks
Floral homage, helpless looked.

Sinfulness too is said to be
The cause of sickness as we see

Forgiveness will restore the health
And it brings back healing wealth.

Sickness coming on sinful wheels
Forgiveness and prayer heals
God who tests our faith through pain
Brings us wholeness once again.

Don't blame others when sickness comes
God our good always wills
Wisdom tells if we bear the pain
God will make us whole again.

Silence and some forbearance sure
With God-given herbs can cure
But when God's time has come to go
We should be prepared also.

100. You Shepherds

Godly shepherds awakened be
Never cast your eyelid once
As your flock is out grazing see
The wolf hides behind the fence.

Wear your staff and your rod in hand
To protect your sheep always
Keep them safe from disastrous land
Lead them through the safest ways.

Walk them to the cool fountain springs
To drink their fill, feel refreshed
Thus they heed to your kind biddings
And thus never feel distressed.

Never leave the weakling small kid
Take it on your shoulder strong
Strain to its body you forbid
And to it give a new song.

When danger comes you stand by them
As their owner give your life
But the bondsman seeing the wolf
Runs away to save his life.

When the evening shadows falling
You gather them together
They know your voice and your calling
Safe into the warm shelter.

This is the way of the Chief Shepherd
The Lord Jesus wants us to
Follow Him as we have harkened
His voice and we serve Him too.

101: The Shepherd

If you are a shepherd
While keeping little sheep
Give green grass to your herd
Take them to shade to sleep.

Hold fast your staff and rod
To draw the straying sheep
And drive the wolf abroad
Safely the flock to keep.

Walk before the sheep to
Call them by quiet call
And lead all of them so
Till they reach your safe stall.

This is what Lord Jesus
The prime Shepherd has told
And He did this for us
So we reach His household.

102. A Pastor's Duties

As you are shepherds of the souls
Do it carefully in intent
For this vocation involves
Fruits that shall shine in the firmament.

Do a good reading of the Word
Never assume you know it all
The more you spend your time with God
The more power your sermon call.

Pray for your people everyday
So the Spirit prepares them well
And their hearts will look for Sunday
Then your harvest will be so full.

Rebuke, set men right for God's sake
God forgives the poor soul that errs
But never does any soul he'll forsake
But His abundant mercy He offers.

Give respect to all your colleagues
You need their prayers in your task
This a saintly man believes
For this gift from God he will ask.

103. Liturgy

Liturgy to the Church a wondrous gift
It is God's great gift to divine worship
Helping us our hearts to heavenwards lift
To sing and praise God with others' fellowship.

Invocation to call worshipper to heed
What a great privilege to us is this
Confession and absolution we need
Guiding us in worship it is great bliss.

End the worship with blessing from altar
Step by step we are guided in the act
With the angels and saints from near and far
As our hearts the heavenly journey start.

Liturgy indeed is a part of our life
Nourishing our souls to eternal life.

104. The Church

The church is not a building
However big and beautiful it be
The Church is a place with people living
A 'church-like' life for others to see.

The Church is not a place to seek
Glory honor and the foremost seat
But servant-hood and life all meek
That's what our Lord had really taught.

The Church is not meant to announce
Our great big works of righteousness
Like the old Pharisee foolishly did once
Telling God much of his godliness.

The church is a place to get forgiveness
Free and abundant by God's grace
And remission too for all our sins
Also then to be counted in His holy race.

But the publican who had instead
Down cast his head in remorse and shame
And knew that he was forgiven indeed
So we should all do the same.

The church is for worship and praise
Thanking God for all that He gave
And to Him both our hands to raise
Imploring Him ever so kindly save.

105. Faith of Our Fathers - 1

Faith of our Fathers great and might
We with Your help with Satan fight
So long as we in the world will live
We to our Lord's Name our witness give.

When we are hungry and be poor
We care for the man next door
Robe the naked to cover his shame
And comfort him in Jesus' Name.

When we are oppressed by the rich
We want to bear patiently such
When in the world we have no name
We have the Name of Christ the same.

When we are denied all comfort
With the faithful we take resort
Living outside the village bounds
Hearing always the heavenly sounds.

We are not sad for all we missed
For reward was to us promised
All that we see is a bubble
But we have a heritage stable.

106. Faith of Our Fathers - 2

Faith of our Fathers
Help us to be true to Thee
As in the sinful world we pass
As darkness all around we see.
        Faith of our Fathers guiding us
        Help us to be true to Thee.

When we were hungry also poor
You have taught us to show mercy

And call the helpless to our door
To give them a morsel taking pity
        Faith of our Fathers guiding us
        Help us to be true to Thee.

Our ancestors were unlettered
Counting on fingers of their hand
Losing their lands for loans battered
Without a shelter to sit or stand
        Faith of our Fathers guiding us
        Help us to be true to Thee.

Faith of our Fathers hope and trust
Kept us alive through all the strife
Bearing the cross in patience must
Go on seeking a better life
        Faith of our Fathers guiding us
        Help us to be true to Thee.

107. When He Called

When He called me to come
I could not see why
But when I simply went to Him
The reason I did not need to try.

When He wanted me to leave
Some comforts of my own
I did not know that He could give
More than the world had shown.

The richest wine and ample bread
Better than I ever seen
He kept on board much ahead
Manna from high heaven.

The nearness of the Lord
And the fellowship of the saints
Was my share and I go forward
With the blessed sacraments.

108. You Give Darshan Before I Seek

Even before I sit to pray
I see my Lord You're already there
Waiting for me and clearly say
That You are not so far away.

Before some words come to my tongue
I hear Thy soothing words so clear
I see all the comfort You bring
And rejoice in the words I hear.

I just seek You with some desire
In feeble faith and ling'ring doubt
But Your countenance like sure fire
Burns my heart and fear goes out.

When Your love to me is so clear
How can I have some doubts again?
As Your voice I so clearly hear
I get assurance, no restrain.

109. Second Plan

Second plan God shows you isn't bad
If you see it like God would rather see
May be in the first one you were glad
But the second can prove better for thee
Accept it without murmur
You may then see the wonder.

Don't seek always the good old place
If it is not for you God's desire
Bithynia comforts and its solace
Are these what you should aspire?
If you want to do God's will
Ask His guidance and be still.

Go to Troas and wait and stand
God sends someone with a plea
To bring the Gospel to western land
That is for you God's plan you see
Is it for you the second offer?
Take it up and you will prosper.

Second offer will not be bad
In fact it will be more blessed
If you accept it you will not be sad
For it is what for you God wanted
Therefore you see in God's providence
The second offer will exceed in excellence.

110. A Fool's Prayer

A fool may pray hours long
It goes only roof high
A broken clock will make big gong
But dumb will be its cry.

A still small cry, repentant moan
Sounds louder than you hear
It reaches inner parts of heav'n
So the Father will sure hear.

God will look for man's inner mind
And hears his repentant cry
Those who seek his mercy will find
And surely will get reply.

111. The Story of the Ladder

You don't need a ladder
To climb the hedge-high bush
Because of course, you are taller
To step on it and easily crush.

Here we have two lessons clear
If we really want to discern in this,
And to give an ear to hear
One is that you are greater than the bush
With heart and soul to seek your God
And follow Him as He would for us wish
And the other is, if there is a will there is a way.

112. Ears to Hear

The wisest man can get it wrong
Some times when he reads the scripture
Surely the certain way to get it right
Is to seek the helping of the Holy Spirit
To get us all the needed guidance
Strangely sometimes we get the message
But it is not always so.

He that has ears to hear
The meaning that the Spirit gives
Will never make it wrong
There are some symbols in the Writ
That will need to be discerned
And the Spirit if we seek
Will surely lead us into Truth.

113. What Do We Seek?

The woman with issue of blood
Lightly touched His garment's end
Did not ask any worldly good
But wanted her sickness to end.

The man at the temple born blind
Did not know what he should have ask'd
But went as told to pool to find
A wonder and his sight received.

The paralytic at the pool
Who did lie there for several years
Carefully he obeyed Christ's call
And his disease then disappeared.

Jairus came to ask nothing but
New life for his daughter who died
Jesus kindly granted him that
Jairus thanked and was satisfied.

The good Roman centurion
Did not think He was truly good
But asked Christ to just heal his man
And that Christ the merciful did.

All these people did only wish
Health and healing to only get
But they did not seek loaves and fish
Which we may easily forget.

114. Seeing and Hearing

The picture that is hanging on the wall
What is that it makes you recall
Is it that made all the kingdoms fade?
Or is that made all oceans dry
Or what it made the heavens brightly awake
I's it the fiery devil that can evil make?

Or all the red bricks that make the wall
What is it that keeps the wall from fall?
All the water cement and mortar
Do they keep it without falling forever?
In the threatening wind and rain and storm
Rolling falling scaling reeling?

This is the song of human pain
The eye to see and the ear to hear
Rocks do not have any of these
Can they ever hear or see.

115. Daily Prayer

The daily prayer is for us like milk
To nourish the inner man to good strength
So we never to sit in prayer sulk
We sit and pray and talk to God at length.

In prayer we sit with Christ side by side
And drink deep His love and the bliss so much
As on the big cloud of Jesus' love we ride
Till the glorious hem of heaven we touch.

We see the countenance of the blessed Lord
And do rejoice to hear His loving voice
Our soul responds willingly to His word
Making us completely deaf to this world.

O, what a joy to sit silent and pray
All our cares and concerns get cast away
Prayer time is a blessed time our way
We rejoice if we sit in prayer day by day.

116. Song of A Little Lamp

In roaring darkness, raging wind
To stand and show His light
The Lord has kept me firm to stand
And to declare His might.

The stormy winds do rise and rage
They cannot quench me sure
His purpose is so strong and wise
His plans ever endure.

The wayfarer and one long lost
Will find his path again
And reach the safe haven at last
Then forget all the pain.

Sinners who have gone astray
Will see my light indeed
To find the way and cast away
All fears and shall succeed.

So let me shine and show the way
To those who need the light
Till at the end they all may stay
In peace, forget the fright.

117. Pilgrims

Blessed are the pilgrims to holy land
Blessed who hold some relics in their hand
Holy sites the saints have trod in the past
Memories with us for a long time last
Places great like holy Constantinople
Places lived by many faithful people.

They built cathedrals and made holy icons
To let the faith live with us through aeons
Where the articles of faith were defined
And the true faith fairly and well proclaimed
And memories were clearly and well laid
Which for our guidance have through long ages stayed.

Jerusalem the city long lasting
Places and paths for us interesting
Kings and emperors had gone to witness
And commemorate sites of blessedness
Bless ye all the name of this holy land
Where our blessed Lord Jesus once did stand.

118. Flowers in the Forests

Once a man in the clan of teachers
And also being a teacher himself
Thought he was so happy and at full ease
Enjoying with his young pupils
Reading from books and climbing trees.

But he was then surely in wrong
And that he knew not he was destined
To a new life that was waiting
A new challenge and a new command
Was he now to take it up or not?
A specific role to play in life's theatre

Life does never come unchallenged
The road ahead is not always smooth and flat
But fields to plough and forests to mend
The teacher's son knew it only slowly.

And one day he found entirely a new place
New place new people to live with
And new tasks and challenges to face
And watch new plants coming to growth
Not dry forests, but flowers in blooming.

The man saw the path threatening at start
And while going steadfast on the path he felt sure
And slowly he found it pleasant and smart
And it also gave him joy which does endure
One does not know what is good till he takes a start.

119. Endless Labor

Life is not all freedom but some discipline
God has not made just as I – but also we
Your freedom to hit will end where my nose begins
All the rules do really end where my safety begins.

One lives a long time and sees a little more
He gathers much experience to his store
And he can lead the horse to the water
But he cannot really make it drink.

Many a prophet had died with a broken heart
Many a guru tried his best wisdom to impart
But life is not a bunch of rules stopping the flow
It is a matter of an ear to hear and heart to obey.

I think when the Lord had made this world
He made a place for good and evil too

Like pouring them to flow each from a different pot
And not so easy to tell those two apart.

After you have tried to make the world good
And have labored to set the good from bad apart
And saw only small progress in doing that
Then you call it a day leave it to God and depart.

120. Your Merciful Visit

Having taken your morning bath
In the rubric rays of the morning sun
You come to me in glorious light
To bring greetings to me for the day.

In the rounded fullness of the moon
On the sixteenth aspect of its life
You come to me my beloved Lord
To let me bask in your peaceful glow.

In the swiftly running lightening path
Which gives me a taste of Thy endless power
Lord, You appear and then disappear
And fill my heart with endless awe.

O Lord, how to tell Your wondrous love
While resting Your wings in the widest realms
You still deem me worthy to make
Your countenance briefly to shine upon me.

121. Our Enemy Fear

Fear is the ancient enemy of mankind
It kills our intention to the right act
It makes us numb and paralyzes our mind
From firm decisions too it can detract.

Fear made Jonah to run away from his task
Fear drove away Jacob to flee from his home
Lot's wife fearing her loss looked back
With fear of death Peter tried to leave Rome.

Fear, they say warns us from coming pain
But often it is fear of the unknown
That drives us to despair again and again
Like even before the storm the ship going down.

Fear not – to His disciples has Christ said
Set your hearts steady and your minds in peace
When storms rise and thunders roaring heard
It is I who is coming to you walking on the waves.

122. Do Not Despair

Do not despair do not fret
For the Lord is with you yet
If you fall in deepest pit
He will lift you now from it

Deep into the forest glade
If you, like a fool have strayed
He will come in search for you
And bring you to safety too

Stormy winds when on you blow
He will stand beside you so
Rain or wind or roaring storm
Will not dare to do you harm

He who had risen from death
Clothes you truly firmly with
Immortality and too
Everlasting life to you

Once his people had to cross
Red Sea and its huge high mass
The almighty raised his hand
Through the sea he showed dry land

If you have the faith to see
God's wonders where you be
Cloudless eye and wholesome ear
These we need to see and hear.

123. He Called Me

Once I was in the wilderness
Searching for the peace I need
But God upon me showed kindness
And called me to him indeed

I thought I knew the way to life
But I knew not I was blind
In the thickness of my hard strife
I thought that the way I found

Just like a long lost son so long
In my sins my soul has died
At last I found that I was wrong
And bitterly cried aloud

God then like a good shepherd came
Found me roaming in the wild
He risked his life to bring me home
Now I am truly his child

And such a great salvation tale
Who can forget it but tell
Night and day on the mount and dale
For his joy and mine as well.

124. The Wanderer

I was wandering
In a wilderness
Lost and forlorn
I could not find the way
Not even a beaten track
Or a trodden footpath.

As I did not know
What to do and where to go
I found a man also like me
Looking out to find a way
I approached him then
Seeking some help
I asked him–Sir, would you show
The way to me to get out
Of this hopeless wicked wilderness.

He then said to me in reply
Friend, I am also like you
Looking for a way to go out
Therefore I'd suggest to you
To try and find the way yourself
And I shall do the same
Myself.

125. Teach Me Forgiveness

Teach me to forgive dear Lord
As you have forgiven me
Teach me to ignore insult
Whoever has done to me

Help me to forget my Lord
Injustice if done to me

Just like it was done to you
When you died on Calvary

Because we are all sinners
Both my opponent and me
If I ask for tooth for tooth
There is not your love in me

You have humbled yourself
And became a poor servant
Sent by God to bear our sins
Salvation through you to grant

The hard virtue, to forgive
Let us all learn at your feet
So we walk in your foot steps
Till in heaven Jesus we meet.

126. Calm Down, Friend

Calm down, dear Friend
You are not the first one in the world
To be ill-treated by the others
It had happened to Great Socrates
And it has happened to Jesus Christ
The other people's estimate.

127. God Bless Moses Kumar!

You are my elder sister's son
And hence so soon my heart you won
Maybe we both sing the same song
As we both walk with God along

You have taken your father's path
To serve the Lord in greater faith
God accepted then your offer
And He made your work soon prosper

The Lord gave you a life partner
Who has guided you in prayer
Your offspring like heavenly stars
Made you twice blessed grand parents

When I wanted a scholar bright
To bring my ministry to light
God has moved your kindly good heart
To join me and sharing your part

I highly praise your scholarship
And your perception, which is deep
I know the Lord blessed your pen
All the *pundits* saw your writings

As you pass your sixtieth mile stone
God will never leave you alone
Making your harvest yet tenfold
Till your crown in your hands you hold

Sixty times sixty be your share
In God's blessing both here and there
Angels do play their harpy strings
Praising God and bring you laurels

Moses this is to you my song
Ringing loud and sweetly along
These my blessings ninety and nine
In the name of your Lord and mine.